The Whole World
Will Rejoice

The Whole World Will Rejoice

New Worship Resources for Justice and Hope

Geoffrey Duncan

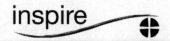

Copyright © Geoffrey Duncan

Cover image © LiquidLibrary

British Library Cataloguing in Publication data
A catalogue record for this book is available
from the British Library

ISBN 978-1-905958-03-0

First published by Inspire
4 John Wesley Road
Werrington
Peterborough PE4 6ZP

Printed and bound in Great Britain by
Athenaeum Press Ltd, Gateshead, Tyne & Wear

Dedication

I look forward to the time when
the whole world will rejoice.
This will include my grandchildren Asha and Maya Patil
along with all the children of the world.

The royalties of *The Whole World Will Rejoice* will be given to
the Down's Syndrome Association, Langdon Down Centre,
2A Langdon Park, Teddington, Middlesex TW11 9PS
www.downs-syndrome.org.uk info@downs-syndrome.org.uk
0845 230 0372

Contents

Introduction

Children and adults die in huge numbers every day – too many to comprehend – from water-related diseases.

People living with HIV/AIDS face appalling suffering, and many die daily. Consider the task facing medical teams and health practitioners in India and Africa.

Climate change and other factors which upset the balance of ecology affect many people. Livelihoods and local cultures are being destroyed across the world. Storm, flood, tsunami, melting ice caps, disappearing species of wild-life, the destruction of rainforests are all facts.

Homophobia is rampant in many places and lives are destroyed. Bullying in the playground and the workplace causes people, including many children, to commit suicide. Consider the prayer 'Remove all prejudice' (page 10).

Many people who go to church would agree with these facts – and the list can be endless – but many of these people 'sit on the fence' when it comes to speaking out about injustice. I believe that in the early twenty-first century the days of remaining in our own backyards and comfort zones are well and truly over. It is long past the time when we should be aware of the true facts and not accept the spin of governments, indeed of anyone who does not wish to answer questions put to them in a straightforward and honest way. We need to research, to be prepared to step out and speak out for justice and peace.

In my dedication I have included, with my two grandchildren, all the children of the world. It is my sincere hope that in this multicultural society and multicultural world we are constantly aware of the precious nature of each individual, starting with children and how they develop as world citizens. Search your mind and ask yourselves questions when reading meditations such as 'Broken Child' (page 48). An inclusive society in which all people are accepted and embraced regardless of colour, culture, sexuality and so-called social standing are essentials for a healthy approach to life. 'If you do not see God in all, you do not see God at all'; a Sikh saying (page 26).

> The whole world will rejoice
> when I am as fault-free
> as I insist you should be . . .

> The whole world will celebrate
> when compassion matters
> more than competition . . .

Norm S.D. Esdon (page 38)

And as Samia Khoury of the Sabeel Ecumenical Liberation Theology Centre, Jerusalem, writes: 'It will be possible for the whole world to rejoice only when there is justice, freedom and peace for all' (page 39).

Geoffrey Duncan
March 2007

Chapter One

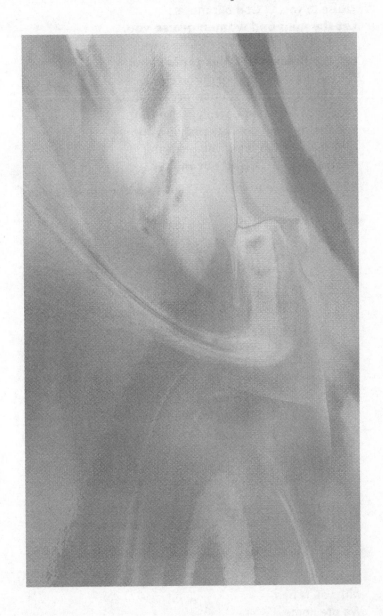

Celebrate our diversity

Praise to you, O God our maker

Praise to you, O God our maker;
Let the men and women praise you.
Let the babes and children praise you;
Let the fields and cities praise you.
Let the dark and daylight praise you;
Let the noise and silence praise you.
Let things seen and unseen praise you;
Let the joy and sorrow praise you.
May our worship bring you pleasure;
Praise to you, O God our maker.

Peter Graystone, England

Gathering prayer

Come, gather
from your homes and health centres
from your schools and shops
from your businesses and banks
from your parks and pubs.
Come, gather
a multicoloured intricate neighbourhood,
a multinational community of God's people.

Clare McBeath, England

With you is home

Star-maker,
Spirit-stirrer,
Story-teller,
with you is home.
We are home;
place of comfort and familiarity.
God forgive us if you become like a slipper or glove and too cosy.
Keep us radical; rooted and real with you and all your cosmos.

Kate Gray, England

A Creed

We believe in a community that opens its doors
    to people who flee war, hunger and poverty
    in search of a better life.

We believe in the power of love, not the power of violence.

We believe that we are called to share our lives
    so as to free each other from poverty, racism
    and oppression of all kinds.

We believe that the resources of the earth
    are to be shared among all people –
    not just the few.

We believe in a community that has as a priority
    a response to those who are denied
    basic human rights and dignity.

We reject a world where people are denied access to warmth,
    food, shelter and the right to live in peace.

We want to believe in justice, in goodness and in people.

We believe we are called to a life of freedom,
    of service,
    of witness,
    of hope.

We reject the idea that nothing can be done.

We believe that a time will come when all people
    will share in the richness of our world,
    and that all people will be truly loved and respected.

We commit ourselves in the name of God
    who created the world for all to share,
    of Christ who leads us to freedom, and
    of the Spirit who calls us to action.

Today we commit ourselves to work together
    to make this belief a reality.

CAFOD, England

Embracing

Loving God, you weave around us your threads of care,
concern and fellowship. You take our differences and
blend them into an intricate pattern where colours merge
and single strands of faith become indistinguishable in
the overall picture of your love. You link us together and
draw us into a circle where we become your body, the
Church in the world in which we live today.
As Jesus used many ways of dealing with individual people,
so our differences in work and worship offer that same
variety of approach. We can never see your design in the
way that you do, but we can learn to trust your guiding
hand so that each strand of faith will play its part in
making the picture complete.
Teach us that, above all else, we must keep on loving.

Marjorie Dobson, England

The joy of intimacy

Tender God, you number the hairs on our head
and count as precious what others deem worthless;
hold us in your care and touch us with your love.

Weave together our lives,
build up relationships of trust
and show us the joy of intimacy.

Deal gently with our hopes and fears,
nurture the people you would have us be
and bring colour to our dreams.

Smile on the work of our hands,
fashion our vision for the future
and fan the wind of change.

Creator God, you make all things new;
challenge the drabness of our lives
and transform our poverty into the riches of your grace.

Annabel Shilson-Thomas/CAFOD, England

Soundscapes of the city

I will sing a new song
of laughter lines etched into old faces
and harmonic hellos overtured across back yards,
the musical melodies of individual lives
soaring counterpoint to the routines of next-door neighbours,
a chromatic community,
a carefully composed concerto
resonating with the soundscape of the city.

I will sing a new song
of unfinished symphonies and silent scores
the cello's E Minor adagio of gut-wrenching pain
grounding the violin's spine-chilling crescendo of crisis,
the pounding of the brass of economic survival,
defiant in anger
discordant with struggle,
resonating with the soundscape of the city.

I will sing a new song,
the sustaining song of the magnificat
of the woodwind's uplifting phrasing
soaring above the mundane backbone of orchestral life;
of the double bass piccatoing its comic solo,
the percussion beating the changing rhythms of the years,
the unresolved cadence of new possibilities
resonating with the soundscape of the city.

Clare McBeath, England

Haiku on the Parable of the Lost Sheep

Shepherd seeks the lost;
ninety-nine are left behind
waiting for the one.

Those who go astray,
wandering, lost and lonely,
Jesus carries home.

No one left outside;
any missing are sought out,
all are wanted here.

A.K. Heathcoat, England

Christ in ordinary people

We praise and thank God for all great and simple joys:
    for the gift of wonder and the joy of discovery;
    for the everlasting freshness of experience;
for the joy of work attempted and achieved;
    for musicians, poets and artisans,
and for all who work in form and colour to increase the beauty of life.

We give thanks for the likeness of Christ in ordinary people,
– their forbearance, courage and kindness,
and for all obscure and humble lives of service.

Glory be to the Father and to the Son.

David Jenkins, England

Images of God

I find my God in the young man who listens
while I cry with anger at the mixed messages
I am receiving from people I need to trust.

I find my God in the women around me
who share with their unfailing
giving to others.

I find my God in the strength of my son
who walked away rather than fight
or stay to be beaten,
even though I needed him to stay.

I find my God in the sister who speaks out,
who won't be silenced by anonymous faces
hidden in decaying structures cemented together
by tradition, whose tradition?

I find my God in the strength of friendship
between people oppressed by society, by physical structures
that keep me out of a building
when churches are open to all!

I find my God in the man who supports me,
fights for me, reflecting his anger,
who takes me where I need to go.

I find my God in the friendship of a woman
who makes time to see me, who believes in me
and loves me;
God is in her eyes and in her heart.

I find my God in the man who delivers my milk,
who is full of energy, in a great hurry,
yet takes the time to pass the time of day
in his own unique and humorous way.

I find my God in the woman who listened and accepted
the words I needed to write,
fragmented God, born of images of need,
not fixed and stuck in tradition,
different for all.

Jean Palmer, England

Remove all prejudice

Loving Lord, it is our hope that our prayers will encircle the world so that there is a better understanding of the needs of all people. We know there are people whose lifestyles are different from ours, we know there are people who live within different cultures. They need to know their own integrity and that they are loved for themselves.

Leader: Two contented men walking hand in hand along the main street attracted abuse from a passer-by who was known to be a supposed pillar of the local church.

People: Loving Lord, as I understand more about the precious nature of each individual I must remove all prejudice from my mind and heart.

Leader: The local Muslim community has been much in the news lately, mostly receiving hate mail.

People: Loving Lord, as I understand more about the precious nature of each individual I must remove all prejudice from my mind and heart.

Leader: One lonely boy, much loved by his family, was not one of the 'in' crowd. Instead he was bullied and beaten by his peer group.

People: Loving Lord, as I understand more about the precious nature of each individual I must remove all prejudice from my mind and heart.

Leader: Single mums keep themselves to themselves at the school gate.

People: Loving Lord, as I understand more about the precious nature of each individual I must remove all prejudice from my mind and heart.

Leader: Refugees flee from the stricken area of Darfur in Western Sudan to start a better life in a neighbouring country.

People: Loving Lord, as I understand more about the precious nature of each individual I must remove all prejudice from my mind and heart.

Leader: The asylum-seeking couple with a one-year-old child are homeless, without food or work. They need urgent help.

People: **Loving Lord, as I understand more about the precious nature of each individual I must remove all prejudice from my mind and heart.**

Leader: Many women, men and children live with HIV/AIDS in African countries and in India. They need modern medication.

People: **Loving Lord, as I understand more about the precious nature of each individual I must remove all prejudice from my mind and heart.**

Leader: Every 15 seconds a child dies from a water-related disease. In developing countries more than one billion people do not have access to clean water.

People: **Loving Lord, as I understand more about the precious nature of each individual I must remove all prejudice from my mind and heart.**

Geoffrey Duncan, England

Dyspraxia

Dear Teacher

I am writing to say how I felt when you said that some people's Dyspraxia is worse than other's. When you said this I felt angry because I don't think that it is right to say that some people are worse than other's. I think that no-one is worse than any one else. I think that we are just all different.

I don't think that Dyspraxia is anything to be ashamed of. I think it just mean's that some people need a bit more help writing like some people need more help with reading than others.

I don't mind having Dyspraxia it hasn't made life difficult at all the only effect it has is that I have to explain why I have my AlphaSmart Laptop which isn't a big deal.

From Joseph Watson, aged 9, England

Letting go

Let go of the day
inhale the silence
release dark into dark
let light seek light.

Withhold nothing
desire nothing
sense weariness
in the stillness.

Know again
inconsistencies
accepting truth
of where you are.

Loving the gift
of who you are.

Eve Jackson, England

Forgiving God,

we come to you
with memories of things which have divided us in the past.
Sometimes these misunderstandings
were based on things that happened long ago
and have been handed down as fully-fledged prejudices.
Sometimes we have been so involved in our own way of doing things
that we have considered any other way to be irrelevant.
Forgive us,
renew us
and give us the courage to think again.

Marjorie Dobson, England

Inviting all

It came to be, in Palestine
    two thousand years ago,
that Jesus – holy Human One –
    set out, that love might grow.
He quickly angered those with power,
    defying priestly rule,
inviting all to join with him
    to ask 'Who is the fool?'

He gathered round for party feasts
    'unclean', excluded folk;
empowered women, lepers, youths –
    the poor laughed with his joke!
For his subversive movement quaked
    the ground the powerful trod:
the lies maintaining wealth with force
    could not confound his God!

The agents of both 'State' and 'faith'
    set out to squash this lord,
whose party shared its life with all,
    whose comrade-spirit soared.
But then, one night, betrayal struck –
    they came with swords and spears
as though expecting violence,
    for Love exposed their fears.

Arrested, 'tried' and crucified,
    the Loving Martyr won:
for though they killed him on that day
    his vision had not gone.
Arisen in re-membered faith
    as we dare share our bread,
inviting all to give it life,
    Love lives! Fear shall be dead!

Tune: Noel or Kingsfold

Graham Adams, England

Lifestyles

Lifestyles so different, all fighting for celebrity,
wanting to dominate and paint over others.

God, empower us to shine brightly
All: **and be the people you created us!**

Lifestyles overpowering our paths and choices,
thinking one lifestyle fits all. One way isn't the only way.

God, empower us to shine brightly
All: **and be the people you created us!**

Colours so different, all fighting for celebrity,
wanting to dominate and paint over others.

God, empower us to shine brightly
All: **all the colours of the rainbow!**

Colours so bold, overpowering pastel shades,
thinking one colour fits all; one colour is all.

God, empower us to shine brightly
All: **all the colours of the rainbow!**

Kate Gray, England

Loving me?

The reason I fail to find love
and be the lover
is because I do not believe.

I do not believe that another
will love me for who I am
and so I fail to risk being vulnerable.
Vulnerable enough to lower my guard
and selflessly be for the other.

It is easier to raise my defences,
naming each 'You' as worthless,
for fear that you first
will sentence me so . . .

Jeanne Blowers, England

14

Diverse ways

God, self-fulfilled in diverse ways,
emergent love, creation's praise,
perfecting nature by your grace:
your image lives in each strange face.

Christ, tendered by strange other hands,
both queer and straight, through all earth's lands:
you loose the fearful from their bonds,
till prejudice, dethroned, absconds.

Impassioned urge to justice shared,
in mutual joy your selfhood bared,
Spirit of heaven: from love you breed
relating bodies, souls to feed.

Strange mystery, erotic power,
disclosed in friendship's fruiting flower,
and on the cross stretched out: for sure,
in love you die, to enrich the poor.

We thank you for all hopes restored,
that strangers will not be ignored;
may every welcome be construed
as your embrace, with love imbued.

May gifts in all each be displayed;
let none by difference be dismayed;
in love's great commonwealth, be lord;
where all serve others, be adored.

Doug Constable, England
with help from the Lesbian and Gay Christian Movement
Hampshire and South Wiltshire branch

Broaden our vision

Vanua God,
we can meet you
through Fijian people and their land-sea love of you.
Broaden our vision of you and our connection with land-sea.

Salsa God,
we can meet you
sensual and spirited, moving with us through Hispanic music.
Broaden our vision of you as we dance through life together.

Truku God,
we can meet you
through ancient songs and instruments of the indigenous Taiwanese
    peoples witnessing on the margins of the church and society.
**Broaden our vision of you as we learn to see you in difference.
Amen.**

Kate Gray, England

The bright wind of heaven

The bright wind is blowing, the bright wind of heaven,
and where it is going to no one can say;
but where it is passing our hearts are awaking
to grope from the darkness and reach for the day.

The bright wind is blowing, the bright wind of heaven,
and many old thoughts will be winnowed away;
the husk that is blown is the chaff of our hating,
the seed that is left is the hope for our day.

The bright wind is blowing, the bright wind of heaven,
the love that it kindles will never betray;
the fire that it fans is the warmth of our caring,
so lean on the wind – it will show you the way.

Tune: The Bright Wind

Cecily Taylor, England

My Creed – My Beatitude

I believe in the precious nature of each individual.
Peace to the people who respect their challenging
and exciting neighbours.

I believe in justice for all people.
Peace to the people who promote just and equal opportunities
for humankind.

I believe in Human Rights for everyone.
Peace to the people who support the right for people
to be accepted for who they are.

I believe in the acceptance of women and men of whatever sexual
    orientation or persuasion.
Peace to the people who speak out against persecution,
bullying, verbal and physical abuse of individuals
    and groups of people.

I believe in an Inclusive Church.
Peace to the people who, with their love and desire
    for the wholeness of humankind, create communities and
    churches where we are enabled to worship
in the spirit of diversity, honesty and love.

Geoffrey Duncan, England

Spirituality

If
our spirituality
is not
life-giving to others
it is not from
God.

It is
of our own making
and speaks
of self indulgence.

Jeanne Blowers, England

17

Reflection on rainbows

Momentary things seen in the sky through rain
need the right conditions to be visible.
Fragile,
cannot be trapped or tamed.
Free, grace-filled beings –
they keep us hoping,
showing us beauty,
catching us unaware and surprising us.

When did we last see a rainbow and look really thankfully on it?

God, we can be your rainbow chasers, led by hints of craziness
    good for the soul.
Rainbow chasers seeking no pots of gold but the treasures of our
    Rainbow God who is wild in the world,
glimpsed here and there.

God, give us eyes to see you, our Rainbow God, painting away
    on the canvas of the world.
Rainbow us, God, so we can paint our towns and villages and cities all your
    colours and see your presence making a difference. Amen.

Kate Gray, England

To be needed

All too often
we call the place
where we feel
most appreciated
the place
where
we are most
needed.

This is not
always so!

Jeanne Blowers, England

Take time

Take this time,
this gift of time,
sink into its depths
of emptiness;
relax into unscheduled space.

Take this time,
time out of time,
to use for your own purpose.
Open again
the door to self,
the individuality of thought
prompted by nothing more
than personal preferences.

Take this time,
space within time,
to stretch
body, mind, imagination,
to re-energize the spirit.

Take this time,
God's time in your time,
to fall in love with life again.

Marjorie Dobson, England

In the temple

(Luke 21.1-14 in the Museum of Science and Industry, Manchester, UK)

In the temple of science, I sat by the turbulence dome: a globe full of shiny custard-coloured stuff which when it is spun round creates beautiful patterns like clouds skimming over a planet like Jupiter. Some children came and wanted it to go faster and others came and wanted it to go backwards. There they were tugging and pulling the planet, making it go in the direction they wanted.

And then a disabled child came up and watched the dome as it spun slowly, gradually, attentive to the changing colour patterns. As it slowed down she tentatively put out her hand and placed it gently on the surface of the globe. As I watched I thought; this is all we have to live on.

Janet Lees, England

Litany of friendship

For as long as you need to know that life is ridiculous,
　　I will laugh with you.

For as long as you need someone to care,
　　I will hold you.

For as long as you need someone to understand,
　　I will weep with you.

For as long as you need to talk,
　　I will listen.

For as long as you need to share silence,
　　I will sit with you.

For as long as you need someone to make life less lonely,
　　I will be with you.

For as long as you need to know that you are valued,
　　I will show you by caring for your needs.

For as long as you need to know that you are worth loving,
　　I will love you.

For as long as you need to know that you make life beautiful,
　　I will smile with you.

To preserve your unique expression of humanity –
　　for as long as you need me,
　　　I am your friend.

A.K. Heathcoat, England

A prayer of confession

**Too many times we are too preoccupied with
our own lives to hear the cries of injustice.**
The cry of the single mother
working night shifts so she can feed her children.
The cry of the cleaning lady who just lost her job,
struggling for dignity
as she lines up for social benefits.
The cry of the young Russian sex worker
who was promised a land of milk and honey
and found only violence.

**We have been too busy thinking
that injustice was far away.**
Forgive us, O God of justice
that we have failed to see
that there is no far away with you.

**Too many times our churches are too preoccupied
with restructuring and household debates,
with numbers and figures,**
to cry out,
to speak up,
to act up.

**We have been too busy thinking
about things that seemed less far away.**
Forgive us, O God of justice,
that we have failed to see
that there is no far away with you.
Amen.

Sonja Rauchfuss, Germany

Conversation

Listening God, you are concerned with our conversations. You hear our sharp debates. You are aware of our differences of opinion. You encourage our attempts at reconciliation. You rejoice when we begin to understand each other and find those links which draw us closer together.

As Jesus debated with his opponents, repeated his teaching for those who were slow to understand and listened to endless problems and questions, so keep our minds open to possibilities we have not yet considered and aware of the challenges we must face as we move forward.

Teach us to be patient in our listening.

Marjorie Dobson, England

How do you play dominoes?

(Dedicated to my dear friend, Janet Lees)

Some people play dominoes,
every move thought out so well,
people can predict one's plan,
and the outcome . . . final!

Others play with dominoes,
standing them in perfect lines,
knocking down the first few,
and watching them fall, one by one.

They sit there to the end,
a must to see each one fall,
and when they all are finished,
the outcome . . . final!

There's very few who set them up
with twists and turns and ends of lines;
they set them off and watch them fall,
then trust in others to keep them going.

With confidence they move on,
knowing they have done their best,
proud of their achievements
but little understood!

Michael Watson, England

Honest Thomas

Bless you, Wise and Holy One,
    for giving us a Thomas;
forgive our slandering him
    as *Doubting Thomas*;
open our eyes, hearts and minds
    to embrace him
    as *Honest Thomas*.

Only Thomas dares to voice
    the craving for proof
    that cowers in the hearts
    of each of the others;
only Thomas dares to show
    his unbelief.

Twice before
    only Thomas is honest
    enough to voice
    what the others
    are too afraid to admit —

When they talk of going back
    to hostile Judea
    to 'awaken' Lazarus,
Thomas voices their unspoken fear:
    'Let us go back to die with him.'
Only Thomas is honest
    enough to admit
    they fear for their own skins, too.

When Jesus assumes they know
    the way to the place he is going,
only Thomas is honest
    enough to say:
    'Lord, we don't know where
        you are going,
    so how can we know the way?'

Bless you, Wise and Holy One,
    for giving us
    Honest Thomas —
for one brave enough
    to reveal what's on his mind
    and in his heart;
for one whose daring
    to ask and to seek
enables us to find
    what we dare
    neither ask nor seek.

Norm S.D. Esdon, Canada

Prayer for renewal

Heal the wounds
of a spirit
so heavy
and I will stir from complacency.

Promise me
the essence
of my possibility
and I will look beyond.

Let me express
a truth
that is not singular
and I will truly see your beauty.

Help me access love
as a necessity
of life
and I will move towards wholeness.

And when we live in a world
where hope
is not a luxury,
then I will dance!

Louise Margaret Granahan, Canada

Guarantees, glory and grit

Lord, forgive us for the times when we feel our lack of faith
    and ask for guarantees on the work we do.
Forgive our lack of trust.
Help us to read the signs that your work is continuing in us.

Lord, forgive us for the times when we look for glory in return for service.
Remind us that Jesus spoke about the first being last.
Teach us true humility, Lord.

Lord, forgive us when we feel like giving up on the struggle to live
    as Christians in a hostile world.
It is not always easy to show grit and determination,
    when everything seems to be against us.
Forgive our human weaknesses, Lord, and strengthen us in troubled times.

Marjorie Dobson, England

Chapter Two

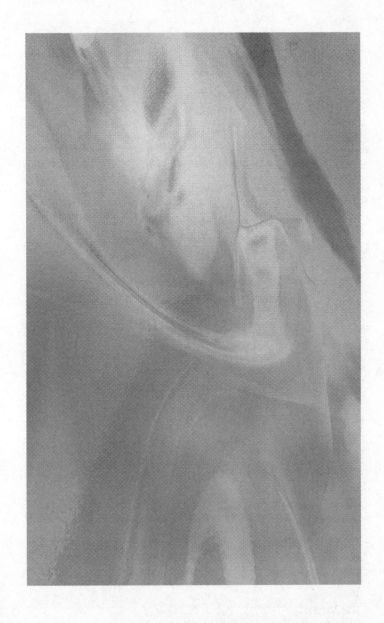

. . . that all might learn

If you do not see God in all, you do not see God at all.

A Sikh saying

God's world

Come to worship
not out of habit
not out of duty
not because your name is on a rota
not because you will earn points in heaven.

Come to worship
because you love God
because you love yourself
because you love God's world
because you love God's people.

We come to celebrate the living God
made present in us and among us.

Clare McBeath, England

A prayer for the love of Christ

Creator God,
source of the universe
and Spirit of life
may I learn to see you
in all things
that as my heart
rises above
my fallen desires
my prayers
will lead me
to
the love of
your Son
Jesus Christ.
Amen.

Andrew Clitheroe, England

Rainbow God

Rainbow God,
who creates all that is,
you bend your church
and shape us into a thing of beauty,
passionate red flaming anger,
vibrant orange dancing sunshine,
deep golden yellow, rich and full,
young, fresh and green,
sad and blue, cool and distant,
moody indigo, dark as the night,
shy violet, quiet violet, forgotten violet.

All the colours are there.
All the colours are here.

Silence

Forgive us,
when we try to paint with one colour,
when everything is tinted with the red of our anger,
when we pick fruit still green,
when our thundery, indigo mood shades out everyone else,
when we ignore the still small voice of violet.
Forgive us our uniformity.
Forgive us our uniformity.
Forgive us our uniformity.

God who puts colours into the rainbow,
paint with us,
weave with us,
plant with us
many colours,
many hues,
one rainbow world. Amen.

Tim Presswood, England

What is God worth?

What is God worth?
We have calculated the value of the life of human beings in compensation cases.
We have even calculated the value of a child based on what it costs to rear one
– tens of thousands of pounds spent on nappies, school books, clothes and food.
And we compare values*:
- one American soldier worth more than one Iraqi civilian;
- the value of British love shown in flowers worth more than a Chilean's health affected by pesticide exposure;
- the loss of a marriage partner in a Soho bomb blast worth more than half a gay relationship.

Human lives, costed, tied up in neat packages, measured.
But what value, really?

What is God worth?
- God who made the Pleiades and Orion, who turns blackness into dawn and darkens day into night;
- God who forms the mountains, creates the wind and dares to reveal thoughts to us;
- God who loved the world so much that the one and only Son was given in order that whoever believes shall not perish but have eternal life;
- God who gave the right to become children of God, co-heirs with Christ;
- The One who chose us before the creation of the world to be holy and blameless;
- The One who marks us with a seal, the promised Holy Spirit;
- God, the Alpha and the Omega, the First and the Last, the Beginning and the End.

What is God worth?
An hour of your time on Sunday and 50p in the collection plate?

These could be altered according to current news.

Jenny Spouge, England

Living Lord of hope for the world

Living Lord of hope,
we spread before you
and before ourselves
petitions, cries and pleas for the people of our world.

In our local area with our church in the midst of diverse communities, we
pray that you will continue to be hope for our church family, our local
community, our world, with all our concerns – emotions . . . sadness . . .
bewilderment . . . joy . . . and immense potential.

We ask that:
　　your love will heal
　　your compassion will deepen our understanding of need
　　your Spirit will guide our actions.

Light a candle for our church community

Living Lord of hope,
in our land of many communities with multicultural, multifaith women and
men we pray that you will educate, inspire and motivate people to be
peacemakers and to encourage leaders, whoever and wherever they may be,
to be informed, diligent and prudent in decision making.

Light a candle for the communities in our land

Living Lord of hope,
in our world and especially at this time, we remember the millions of refugees,
including the starving children in refugee camps worldwide, who are trying to
pick up the pieces of their once-peaceful lives. We know that each one of them
is different from the other but with hope connecting each of them we pray for
a better future and a chance to restore lasting peace to their lives.

As Eleanor Roosevelt quoted:
　　'It is better to light a candle than to curse the darkness',

so we light candles for some of the countries and peoples where, in this
war-torn world with power, greed and money as the gods, we remember
the women, the children, the men who suffer in Iraq, Iran, North Korea,
Sri Lanka, Afghanistan, Palestine and Israel.

Light candles for parts of our world

Living Lord of hope, enable us in our own individual God-strengthened,
peace-loving lives to keep the flame of hope alive for everyone. Amen.

Geoffrey Duncan, England

Bearing pain

How much pain, Lord,
hidden in the group around this table?

One, steel-corseted as a boy, unable
to play boys' games with other boys;
one whose little son drowned tragically;
another whose wife died young;
illnesses borne quietly,
miscarriages mourned silently,
marriages broken jaggedly,
losses grieved tearfully.

How much pain, Lord,
hidden in hearts, undisclosed?

Pain of failed exams or ventures,
pain of unreached goals and dreams,
pain of another's disdain or rebuff,
pain of incestuous abuse,
pain of being on the outside of an in-group,
pain of wasted years and lost hope,
pain of unconquered addiction,
pain of inability to lessen another's pain.

How much pain, Lord,
hidden to ward off vulnerability?

There's too much pain for me, Lord,
in this pain-bedevilled world.
I cannot cope with the knowledge
of starving thousands and mine-crippled kids;
of bombs obliterating schools, hospitals and churches;
of leaders enjoying luxury built on the corpses of their people;
of neighbour killing neighbour and adults raping children;
of unjust imprisonment and denial of all human rights.

How much more pain, Lord, can you bear?

I've already borne it all, my child.

Abigail Joy Tobler, England

A fairer world

Lord God, who sent your only Son, Jesus Christ, to our world that we may all live as one in him, help us to see that it is our duty to consider our brothers and sisters in the struggling parts of the world; to help others who are in need, even of the basic things in life. Forgive us for exploiting them as we look for cheaper goods and teach us to consume less. May we remember to buy products which have been traded fairly, products which may be a bit more expensive for us, but will make all the difference to the lives of others. Let us know that we will not be giving to those people, but giving back that which is rightly theirs, even as we rightly demand a decent wage.

We pray for all people living in slavery, especially little children forced to spend their childhood working. All day and every day, children as young as four years old, many with empty bellies, work in sweatshops, down mines or on stinking garbage heaps, picking up rags or bits of plastic to sell for a pittance, because their families are living in poverty. Lord, help us to honour life and not to exploit it, whether it be human life or the rest of your creation, and we ask that slavery may be fully abolished in our time. Through Jesus Christ our Saviour, who came that all might be free. Amen.

Elizabeth Smith, England

Confession

God, I'm in deep;
there's nowhere else to turn,
lift me out.

God, this place is in deep;
I don't know if we have a future here.
God save us.

God, this world
is in deep;
all of us are in it,
all the structures, powers;
we are all in it.
Sin? Debt?
We are in it.
Give us hope.

Bob Warwicker, England

Weaving prayer

In the still watches of the night
monks, in buildings of stone
built to your glory,
faithfully joined in prayer.
The threads of Christianity
drawn across the centuries
stretching back in time
and rolling out ahead of us into the future.

And we who join in prayer,
this night, in this place,
are part of the pattern
woven into your design,
the tapestry of your people,
the faithful and those us who struggle to be faithful.
Did they find faith any easier, those who came before us?
Will they find it any easier, those who follow us?
Will our part of the pattern inspire them
as those who've gone before inspire us?

And as dawn breaks
in threads of pink across the sky,
we see your faithfulness to us.
The sun rises,
the earth turns,
balanced, finely tuned.
And we realize the magnitude
of the needs of this world.
Countries and people of whom we know so little.
Unlike us and yet so like us.
Your children, created in your image.
Do they know that our prayers reach out to them this night?
Do theirs reach out to us?
Threads across the miles
as well as through the passing of time.
May this cloth we weave together
cover your earth
and enfold it in peace and love.
And may your kingdom come. Amen.

Jenny Spouge, England

Petition

God, creator,
help us to create ways of relating
financially
that make the best use of your good
earth,
and of human talents,
that don't destroy people,
but build them up.

God, servant,
give energy to all who work
to relieve debt.
Give wisdom to people who decide
for international banks or local credit
unions,
for mortgage lenders or
microlenders,
who gets money and who doesn't.
Give power to all
whose life's work is to heal
the spirit wounded by debt.

(God, spirit,
bless all our relating
with something greater than equity;
bless it with love.)

Bob Warwicker, England

Bring an end to injustice

Lord God, I pray for all who risk their freedom to draw attention to evil. Protect
the lives of all who stand against dishonesty or call corrupt leaders to account.
Prosper all those who use godly means to bring an end to injustice, and work
in the hearts of those who have done much that is wicked to bring them to the
point where they recognize the need to change. Amen.

Peter Graystone, England

Meditative prayer

And the children came,
boisterous, free-spirited,
no preconceptions,
enjoying just being,
and you said,
'The kingdom of heaven is theirs.'

A rich man came,
one of the world's success stories,
a high flyer,
an achiever,
shelves stacked with glittering prizes,
and you said,
'Give it away,
because you've lost what the children have got.'

Lord,
it's so easy to lose the kingdom,
so easy to clutter life up,
and make the simple complicated.

So lead us to the simplicity of life with you.
Open our eyes and show us how near we are to your kingdom,
for it brushes our sleeve,
as children play, and the rain drips from the branch,
as laughter breaks the tensions, and the smell of fresh bread
permeates the house.

Take away the barriers,
stop us from falling into rich-young-man syndrome,
and being so rich, so religious, so clever that we lose sight of you,
our simple, gracious, loving God.
Grant us the grace to set free the child within us,
for we ask it in the name of the one who welcomed the children. Amen.

David Cornick, England

Just an ordinary man

(Dedicated to Bob Geldof)

Just an ordinary man –
scruffy at that,
unshaven chin,
and a battered old hat;
he felt his giving worthless
and so it all began,
for he became a catalyst
that ordinary man.

There's a whole lot of treasure
locked in people's hearts –
that's the kind of place
where a vision can start;
where miracles of loving
are multiplying bread
with everybody joining in
the hungry can be fed.

Just an ordinary man
made us think again
on the cause of want
and the famine of grain,
and does the world spend money
to do the best it can?
We'll go on asking questions like
that ordinary man;
we'll try to help remembering
that ordinary man.

Cecily Taylor, England

Once more

Once more, Lord, I struggle
with the words which say you satisfy
the hunger and thirst of every living thing,
showering your abundance on them.

And yet, once more, we hear
of deaths through famine,
of conflicts which ravage the land
and mutilate the people.

Where Lord, is your abundance for them?
Where your compassion and grace?
Where your faithfulness and kindness?
Where?

Once more I struggle, Lord,
with faith which believes your goodness
and world reality which does not experience it.
The tension is almost unbearable.

Abigail Joy Tobler, England

Transformation

God's inexplicable power transforms
the crucified defeated Jesus,
the broken recipient of humanity's worst hatred,
into the glorified risen Lord,
beyond the scope of human evil,
calling us to come into his realm of love.

God's inexplicable power transforms
very ordinary powerless people,
even those burdened with wrongs,
inflicted by self or others
into glorified wholeness
if we come with open hearts.

Ros Murphy, England

And when will the whole world rejoice?

(A congregational chant)

All: **And when will the whole world rejoice?**
When millennium goals are met.

All: **And when will the whole world rejoice?**
When fresh water flows freely.

All: **And when will the whole world rejoice?**
When slow food replaces fast food.

All: **And when will the whole world rejoice?**
When all people have enough.

All: **And when will the whole world rejoice?**
When all people know themselves to be loved.

All: **And when will the whole world rejoice?**
When wars for oil have ceased for good.

All: **And when will the whole world rejoice?**
When no one lives in fear or despair.

All: **And when will the whole world rejoice?**
When heaven and earth meet and the way of God's community includes all.
Let's continue to walk along God's way together today,
so that the whole earth will rejoice.
Amen. Amen!

Kate Gray, England

The world rejoices

God, allow us to tell our stories,
let the world hear the facts.
Give us opportunities to share our testimonies,
let the world hear the truth.
Encourage us to overcome the barrier of silence,
let the world hear voices, loud and clear.
Strengthen us to speak with indignation,
let the world hear and weep.
Comfort us to pursue justice and mercy,
let the world hear courage and determination.
Help us endeavour to forgive our trespassers,
let the world rejoice with us.
God, allow us to tell our stories.

Frances Ballantyne, England

The whole world will rejoice (1)

The whole world will rejoice
    when I am as fault-free
    as I insist you should be;
    when we view our enemy
    as estranged family;
    when left-wing and right-wing
    work together
    to fly the dove
    beyond the reach of
    the rockets' red glare.
The whole world will celebrate
    when compassion matters
    more than competition;
    when we listen to the stock-taker
    as religiously as we cater to
    the stockholder;
    when we are as quick to spot
    the root-of-evil in ourselves
    as we are
    the axis-of-evil in others.
The whole world will dance
    when beluga and caribou
    peregrine and pine
    can bless the day
    Adam was born;
    when Adam and Eve
    can leave
    their solitary confinement
    to live together
    in every single human.
On that day
    the morning stars
    shall sing together
    and all the trees of the field
    shall clap their hands.

Norm S.D. Esdon, Canada

The whole world will rejoice (2)

It will be possible for the whole world to rejoice only when there is justice, freedom and peace for all. But when the powerful abuse the powerless, and the rich abuse the poor and the strong abuse the weak, there will not be much rejoicing around the world.

One of the most important ministries of our work at Sabeel, since its inception, has been the ministry of justice and peace. Yet every day seems to be getting further away from achieving peace or guaranteeing any justice.

While there is plenty for everybody's need, there certainly isn't enough for everybody's greed. So we watch material greed reaching out to deplete natural resources and ruin the whole environment. We watch the greed for power, and feel so helpless against the powers of domination that are in control, and determining the destiny of peoples around the world. Over and above, those powers have marginalized the role of the United Nations, the international body which was created to solve conflicts, and to guarantee justice, peace and freedom for all. We watch wars waged under false pretexts, and we watch the moral values around us going down the drain, and then we wonder why the world is in such a mess. But do we give up? Certainly not, because we believe in a God of Justice who will 'set all free'.

> 'When he was abused, he did not return abuse; when he suffered, he did not threaten; but he entrusted himself to the one who judges justly' (1 Peter 2.23).

Both Christian and Muslim Palestinians have this trust based on a deeply rooted faith where God is revealed as a God of Justice not only in the Bible, but also in the Koran.

Samia Khoury, Sabeel Ecumenical
Liberation Theology Centre, Jerusalem

The world will rejoice

God of passionate commitment to the poor, and especially to children, help us to bring rejoicing to your whole creation.

We thank you for your silence to the groaning prayers of Jesus in the Garden of Gethsemane, may it be a particular challenge to those of us who are affluent Christians;
O God of love,

All: **With Jesus we pray.**

May we dive deeply into the pool of your silence in times of extreme tragedy, especially when it involves the death of innocent indigenous children;
O God of love,

All: **With Jesus we pray.**

May we live in your silence, dying to false security, false theologies and false Christian joy;
O God of love,

All: **With Jesus we pray.**

May we face the outrageous outcomes of a passionless church and nation;
O God of love,

All: **With Jesus we pray.**

May we move from guilt at our communal complicity to commitment to social justice as the core of your gospel;
O God of love,

All: **With Jesus we pray.**

May we stop compromising the gospel of inclusiveness, and reclaim liberation from oppression;
O God of love,

All: **With Jesus we pray.**

May we discover a daily spirituality in which we live to die, and die to live, in a continuous cycle of resurrection living;
O God of love,

All: **With Jesus we pray.**

May we find energy and companions to work towards transformation of the systems which we as Pakeha* have created;
O God of love,

All: **With Jesus we pray.**

May we stop worrying about the survival and unity of the Church and nation, and dismantle greed and the need to control those who are different from us;
O God of love,

All: With Jesus we pray.

May we become non-violent uncomfortable stones in the shoes of the Church and State when our actions continue to attack the poor, the vulnerable and marginalized;
O God of love,

All: With Jesus we pray.

May we become disobedient subverters of the Church when it tries to smother its own prophetic voices, and colludes with State policies that protect wealth and enslave the vulnerable;
O God of love,

All: With Jesus we pray.

May we find new forms of church and community in which the tomb remains empty, setting free the exploding new life of an immanent, vulnerable God who will not be contained by dogmas and confessions of faith;
O God of love,

All: With Jesus we pray.

Vulnerable, silent God, challenge us as affluent Christians to re-discover resurrection living so that all your children are housed, fed, healthy and safe from fear and abuse;
O God of love,

All: With Jesus we pray.

May we become lavish in hospitality to those whom we have marginalized, that we may all find hope and genuine rejoicing.

All: Amen.

* White New Zealanders

Jean Brookes, Aotearoa New Zealand

Song of the vineyard Eucharist

How can I sing a song of my vineyard
when the earth lies tattered and in ruins?
War rages, not once but in country after country;
bombs rip apart idyllic holiday destinations.
Floods destroy the old Latin Quarter,
home to musical memories and artistic flare.
Politicians meet to keep at arm's length
the country that bridges East and West, Muslim and Christian.
Reports from feeding camps in Africa become a forgotten memory
but hunger and disease rage unabated.

How can I sing a song of my vineyard
when the vines lie in tatters, ripped from the earth?
I have given my vineyard the best of everything,
tended it with sun and rain,
but its fruits are small and withered, disease is rife.
I looked for good fruits
but you have produced a poor harvest;
the produce you should have enjoyed
lies rotting in the ground.
How can I sing a song of my vineyard?

But I will sing a song of my vineyard;
the earth is more resilient and beauty radiates!
My tangled tomato plants grow robustly skywards
and the small green fruits are swelling with promise.
Sudan's people take the long road south,
returning to their ancestral homelands to build their children's future.
A film festival is held in a small theatre in war-torn Baghdad;
awards are presented accompanied with bouquets of flowers.
And families open their homes and make up spare beds
for the survivors of Hurricane Katrina's devastation.

But I will sing a song of my vineyard,
a song of my beloved who gently tends the vine!
Who feeds and waters and lifts the shoots out of the dust,
splicing the vine together with words of encouragement.
My beloved, who on the night the vines became gnarled and twisted,
ensnaring him and betraying him, fearful of a beautiful garden,
took bread, the labour of the harvest,
and broke it for the vineyard, dust to dust, ashes to ashes;
took wine, the fruit of the vine,
and poured out his blood to enrich the soil.

Share bread

This is my body, broken for you.

Share wine

This is my blood poured out for the life of the world.

And what became of the song of my vineyard,
the song of my beloved now buried in the ground?
My beloved's love could not die, could not lie hidden,
it springs from the ground, pushing up through the soil.
Life pulses through the vineyard, flowers blossom,
bees hum and birds sing in celebration.
Ruined vines are once again tended with patience,
broken trusses lovingly spliced back onto the vine.
The fecundity of the vineyard embraces the brokenness,
and the grapes are sweet and ripe and ready for the harvest.

Clare McBeath, England

Beyond Make Poverty History

God of our past, present and future,
look with compassion on the wrong we have done,
deal gently with who we are,
and fire us up to become the people you would have us be.
Grant us humility to learn from the past,
courage to embrace the present,
and wisdom to change the future,
that we may press on to make poverty history.
Make us mindful of our achievements,
ever eager to work for justice
and always ready to do your will
that your kingdom may come on earth.
Give us energy in the wake of apathy,
inspiration in the face of opposition
and hope in the path of despair,
that poverty may find an end
and humanity discovers a new beginning. Amen.

Annabel Shilson-Thomas/CAFOD, England

43

Not quite

This is not quite the last water from our well.
This is not quite the last crop we shall sow.
This is not quite the last aid we'll be given.
This is not quite the life I had dreamed of for my family.
This is not the worst of it or the best of it,
surviving on the brink of not quite enough,
balancing between weary and grateful –
with not quite enough life in between.
Some days . . . only some days I find myself thinking
this is not quite fair.

Eve Jackson, England

God of the waters

God of the waters,
may all who call out to you in thirst
find what they seek:
clean water to those in physical need;
living water to those in spiritual need. Amen.

Peter Graystone, England

Illumine our hearts and minds

Illumine our hearts and minds,
O Gethsemane God,
that we may watch and pray with those who weep.
Kindle within us a fire for justice
that we may hold fast to your truth
and ever seek to make poverty history.
Remove the barrier of apathy
that we may reach out to the oppressed
and fly your flag for freedom.
Passionate God, ignite us with your resurrection spirit
that flickers of despair become flames of hope
and darkness gives way to light. Amen.

Annabel Shilson-Thomas/CAFOD, England

Running sores

How can I turn my back on you
beggar child?
I see your twisted legs
running with sores,
red and glistening on the brown
of dirty skin;
If only I could wash and bind
those running sores,
feed that starving belly,
hold that withering frame –

But who am I –
an onlooker
who came but idly to observe,
brushing away flies,
sidestepping dirt,
and drinking only bottled water
on my way?

Can I hold the whole world
in my arms,
bind up its sores
and feed its starving belly?
Can I change a single thing,
bring any sort of equity
unto the people of the earth –
can I make any difference?

I think not . . .

For my own small life holds
no significance –
none more or less than yours –
for you and I are specks upon the spectrum
both –
but I can at least try –
and that is my promise to you,
beggar child –
that is my promise.

Margot Arthurton, England

Children of a lesser God

My journey is on and the road is long
upon the rugged land and
into remote villages.
I keep meeting men and women
with dry cracks on their tired faces.
They walk through life quietly.
Their cries are silent and
their pain is deep.
They are God's special people.

Marked forever to be marginalized
by the rich and the powerful.

My journey is on and the road is steep.
I keep seeing faces
that haunt my thoughts.
Looking for an answer.
I see their bodies broken with the harshness of reality.
They live each day through hunger and thirst.
Their eyes have lost hope
as they remain the outcast
at the fringe of the village.
Their tears stay hidden behind poverty.
No one dares listen to their whisper
and there is no sign of freedom for these deserted folk.

My journey gets harder,
and the heat unbearable.
I drive through miles
of treeless, barren land
that is being abused by the greedy.

Here the children of a lesser God have opened their doors
to the so-called 'development pundits'
who came in the guise of 'saviours'.
They promised 'milk and honey',
and preached about equity.
They have only proved to be agents of 'globalization',
who create wider disparity
between rich and poor,
and speed up the process of a global catastrophe,
self-destruction of humanity,
while they celebrate their new found riches
in foreign lands.

M.R. Manohar, South India

46

God is dying with the children

God is dying with the children,
sunlight filters through the haze.
Actions of retaliation
shatter, damage, scar and craze.

Blind to this annihilation,
should we simply wring our hands?
Is the carnage that we witness
something mercy understands?

Should we pray that God will hear us,
bring an end to human strife?
But the choice is ours for action:
we should choose, choose now, choose life.

So our prayers are prayers for courage,
facing those who maim and kill,
standing with the weak and helpless,
as we seek to do God's will.

We would join the wounded healer,
we would risk the rage of friends,
living out the love of Jesus,
knowing love that never ends.

Andrew Pratt, England

. . . that the rich might learn from those who are poor

Lord,
let those of us who live in luxury
learn from those who do not
for while they will always be with us
our worldly wealth will not.
For we know that our souls will not be saved
by clever sermons or sleight of hand
but by silent and reverent service
of the poorest in the land.

Andrew Clitheroe, England

A prayer for solidarity

God of grace,
creator of a world of plenty,
the heavens declare your glory
and the earth your generosity.
In love, you created us
and in your likeness you made us
to be partners in creation.
In greed, we have turned away
and have marred your image in us
to fashion a fragmented world.

Renew in us your vision of wholeness,
that the rich may restore wealth to the poor
and the poor share blessings with the rich.
Revive in us a passion for justice,
that the tyranny of profit be quelled
and whispers of freedom find voice.
Refresh in us our sense of calling,
that we may follow Christ in serving others
and live simply with those who simply live.

Annabel Shilson-Thomas, England

Broken child

This is the story of a special child,
from the barren lands of North Karnataka
where people live at the mercy of God,
an extreme climate where
the land is dry
and a morsel of food a gift from heaven.

This is the reality of a lonely child dressed in rags.
When just a baby she lost her mother and
now she's battered by her third
stepmother
who punishes her each day for
her limited potential
to bring home bread for the family.

She was raped
by her own.
Her grand old man.

Fighting,
between life and death
she birthed a baby
and lost it soon after
to the open arms of death.

She cries in silence, she cries all alone;
Unheard in the harshness of the world.

This is the truth of a little child.
Her voice is lost in the wilderness.
Who dares listen to this cry?
Some days when her pangs of hunger get painful
she flees to the hills.
She speaks to the trees for comfort
and fills her stomach with leaves and wild berries.

She is a broken child
crying out
for someone to reach her
to love her.
Her little eyes and her small body have seen too much
of life.
She carries bruises and pain for no fault of hers.
Her heart aches for love and yet
she survives
each day with an indomitable will.

She is a broken child.
She is a special child.

M.R. Manohar, South India

Find room

In the night,
women wait.
Bridegroom comes
to the gate.
Lamps are lit,
some too late
for the time of greeting,
so they miss the meeting.

> *We will watch and pray*
> *for his coming day*
> *and we trust,*
> *as he comes,*
> *he will find us waiting.*

In a cold
stable stall
lay a child
for us all,
but so few
came to call
on the baby stranger
lying in that manger.

Chorus

On a cross
on the hill
Jesus died,
stranger still.
Priests were out
for the kill,
and that power would show him
that they did not know him.

Chorus

In our time,
will he come?
Will our lives
find the room
for the one
in whose home
we receive a greeting,
love and judgement meeting?

Chorus

Tune: Theodoric and refrain

Marjorie Dobson, England

Parent, forgive

Uniting God, we pray for forgiveness that we frequently fail
to reflect your life of love. Forgive us our part in the divisions
between nations, and for divisions between those people we
know and love whom we hurt or ignore.

Help us celebrate the diversity of cultures, genders
and creeds, and to recognize our part in
combating inequality and discrimination.

We pray for solutions to problems that divide us –
so that the gap between poor and wealthy,
between sick and healthy, may be bridged.

Enable us to initiate further action to encourage, and ensure,
that inequities in world trade continue to be tackled, and
ultimately overcome for the millions of poor people who seek
a better future for themselves and their children.

We pray for development of policies of eco-justice and, dear
God, lead us to a day when differences and diversity
are no longer seen as sources of division and distrust,
but of strength and inspiration.

Steer us toward positive attitudes, and relationships of
mutual respect that cross boundaries, and result in bringing
fullness of life and justice to all – in our shared world.

Teach us to use opportunities, offered through One World
Week and other relevant events, to learn about the widening
gap between rich and poor and, together,
take informed action for justice.

In Christ's healing name we pray.

Wendy Whitehead, England

A prayer for forgiveness

Dear God, forgive me for the times I have turned my back on you and forgotten you in those I have met today. For my materialism have mercy, in my spiritual growth grant strength and in my nakedness cover me with your love. Amen.

Andrew Clitheroe, England

Jesus on the boundaries

Jesus on the boundaries
of our social living,
welcomed taxmen, prostitutes:
they rejoiced, believing,
took the first seats at his feast
bread and wine receiving,
brought within the loving world
of his total giving.

Jesus breaks the boundaries:
'Bring the children to me.'
Hails a sinning woman's gift:
'Good this thing you do me.'
Tells the hopeless, humble folk:
'Find the Father through me.'
Comes in hungry, thirsty, sick:
'Serving these, you knew me.'

Jesus, break our boundaries,
our closed lives extending.
Put an end to us and them,
giving, and not lending.
Greeting loveless in your name,
envoys of your sending,
we will join a loving world,
kingdom never ending.

John Lansley, England

The kiss of life

(A whole-world just-health)

It was a particular treachery that had Judas betray his
Lord with a kiss. Perhaps he was cowardly – perhaps,
even then, he was trying not to implicate himself:

kissing rather than pointing.

But, be that as it may, it was still a 'kiss of death'.

We have a 'kiss of life'. Paul tells us that we are
entrusted with the ministry of reconciliation: sharing in
the life-giving that brings . . . a 'kiss of life'.

In evocative words from the Iona Community, we are
asked, 'Will you kiss the leper clean?' The community
might just as easily have written, 'Will you kiss the
AIDS patient clean?' Or, more generally,
'Will you kiss the outcast clean?'

We have a kiss of life.

Our calling is to embrace the world and not fear being
embraced by the world: finding Christ in the face of the
poor and the prince; moved to work for justice: to live
the love of Christ for the world.

A kiss of life, a breath of renewal, a shared rising.

Don't point! Kiss! Don't betray! Embrace!

Stephen Brown, Scotland

Go forth from this place

Leader: Go forth from this place an awakened people,
aware of the world's brokenness,
yet committed to its wholeness.

People: We are reminded of God's will for unity in the world.

Leader: Go forth from this place an inspired people,
aware of the fragmentation of our faith communities,
yet working towards reconciliation.

**People: We are reminded of Jesus' prayer for unity of all
who believe in him.**

Leader: Go forth from this place a challenged people,
aware of your call to serve together
beyond boundaries.

**People: We have heard the good news;
we have been empowered to share it;
we commit ourselves as witnesses to it.**

Hope S. Antone, Philippines

Wisdom

We are called to share the earth with other species;
Aborigines, Inuit, Sami, all know this wisdom.
Yet we plunder and expand beyond sustainable limits,
raking sea beds, drowning circumnavigators,
chopping down the homes of our nearest relatives*
forcing herbivores and carnivores alike to the margins.
Forgive us, generous Creator,
as we redouble our efforts to conserve and adapt.
Help us to see that without biodiversity
our days are numbered.
May we rediscover the value and respect for creation
that causes your first people to name them so wonderfully.

*The circumnavigators are albatrosses that drown when hooked by long-line
fishing. Our nearest relatives are the apes: gibbons, orangutans, chimpanzees
and gorillas, all declining due to our cutting down of their habitat.*

Janet Lees, England

Chapter Three

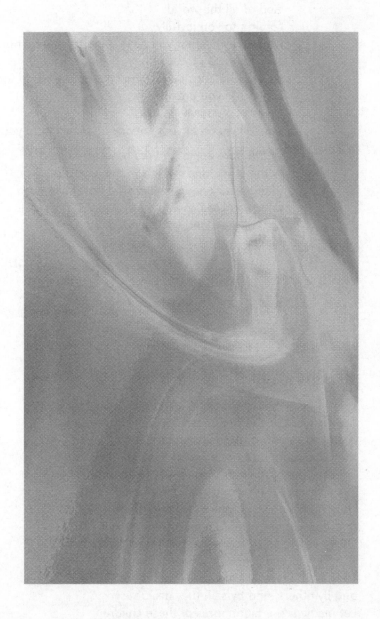

Take hope – know joy – witness justice

God of all the world

God of all the world:
coming to you joyfully,
we celebrate what you have done to change our lives;
coming to you thankfully,
we stand alongside all who change the world for good;
coming to you prayerfully,
we offer ourselves in love.
May all we do in your service be pleasing to you.

To the bare earth that we have exhausted,
to the stark lands which we have stripped,
to the weary people whom we have dismayed,
return, O Lord,
with blessed and refreshing joy.
Amen.

Peter Graystone, England

The stories of the children

Let me hear the stories of the children.
They are not tales from books that they have read.
If they were only make-believe and fiction
they would not have made a mess inside their head.
They tell me of the fear they feel at night-time.
They close their eyes and keep their body furled.
They cry inside so no one ever hears them,
and they cannot comprehend a bright new world.
They need to know someone has heard their story.
They're sad and scared and lonely and ill-used.
They live a life where no one wants to love them,
and by others, and by self, they are abused.
Let me hear the nightmares of these children,
help me give them strength when that abuse is hurled.
Give them ways to open doors to freedom,
so they glimpse, feel, and find their bright new world.

Fredwyn Hosier, England

Love, joy, hope

'I am the vine, you are the branches. Those who abide in me and I in them bear much fruit.'

'This is my commandment, that you love one another as I have loved you.' (John 15.5,12)

Nobody knows how many street children – mostly boys and some pregnant girls – there are in Lima, capital of Peru. It could be as many as 300,000. They are known locally as 'gutter rats'.

The Vine Trust is a Scottish based charity that over the last 10 years has worked to rescue as many of these street children as it can. Charity workers have funded several homes, schools and educational projects and set up business ventures that provide funds and work for older boys and girls.

They have also acquired two ex-naval supply vessels and have fitted them out as hospital ships – called Amazon Hope 1 and 2. They sail up and down the Peruvian stretch of the Amazon River, treating and supporting the poor families who live on its banks. They are staffed by volunteer medical parties from Scotland, each one working a two-week stint, and they treat up to 2,000 people in 10 days. The hope is that by doing this they can help the families before they reach the desperation point of turning their children out on the streets.

Why 'gutter rats'?
We live in the sewers and
   come out at night
letting our bodies be misused
just to get some food;
sometimes we are so hungry we
   even eat earth.

Thrown out by my family because
they couldn't afford to keep me;
I sniff cheap glue to try and
   rub myself out
and make myself disappear;
I will soon be dead anyway;
if I do not starve I will be
   kicked and beaten
or shot by the police.

But one day someone came
   and took me
to a place where there was food
   and clothes
and a real bed to sleep in.

Now I am surrounded by kindness –
   not cruelty,
I am respected – not despised,
I am held by arms that comfort me –
not gripped by arms while they
   abuse me.
I don't wake each day wanting to die;
I go to school,
I play football.

My whole life is filled with
love
joy
hope

Heather Johnston, Scotland

Rejection

Unemployment is always there.
So is loneliness,
sadness, fear,
poverty and pain,
doubt, despair,
addiction,
loss and bereavement.
Saying goodbye is always there.
So is bullying,
failure, rejection,
helplessness,
hopelessness,
breaking down
and breaking up.
Always there.
Being too young,
being too old,
not being wanted,
always there.
On the streets,
the sick-bed,
behind bars,
between four walls.
Up the spout,
the creek
without a paddle.
Always there.
Life and death,
always there.
The love of God,
always there.

Fredwyn Hosier, England

TRC

(Truth and Reconciliation
Commission)
Silent letters on silent stones
spelling the names of those
no longer with us
spirited away from loved ones
without any warning
bludgeoned and bulleted
    into oblivion
by nameless state-funded minions.

Silent hurts
continue the killing
silently inhabiting
the memories
of loved ones.

Then a new dispensation
and the silence is broken
in a flood of words
fleshing the hurts
now exposed for the healing
as truth painfully surfaces
and faces unseen are now seen
to give meaning to the misery.

Now silent letters on silent stones
sound in singing
of the names of those
no longer with us.

Harry Wiggett, South Africa

58

Abuse is . . .

Abuse is power,
power to change someone else's
    thoughts,
power to reduce them to rubble.

Abuse is fear,
fear of never being loved,
never being good enough.

Abuse is fear,
fear of consequences,
fear of pain.

Abuse is secrets
and lack of privacy
and invaded space.

Abuse is time,
making others late,
proving your own power.

Abuse is hidden,
leaves no mark,
cannot be proven.

Abuse is avoiding responsibility,
blaming me;
everything is my fault.

Abuse is feeling unable to change,
too weak to fight,
too useless to win.

Abuse is not being taken seriously,
being laughed at,
being belittled.

Abuse is feeling dirty,
Feeling unlovable,
feeling useless.

Abuse is being shit-scared,
so scared that you daren't say no
to things you know will hurt,
to things that are wrong.

Abuse is looking at the ceiling
and praying that it will soon
    be over,
or wishing he would die now.

Abuse is waking up
and swearing and crying
because you haven't died,
and neither has he.

Abuse is words,
words that haunt
and tease.

Abuse is violence,
lack of respect,
lack of space.

Abuse is destructive,
destroying someone else,
destroying life.

Abuse is wishing you were dead
because it sure beats being alive.

A Survivor, England

What am I worth?

What am I worth,
a smack round the head,
and saying I'm useless,
and wishing me dead?

What am I worth,
a chain on the door,
and kicking me senseless
when I'm on the floor?

What am I worth,
a bundle of nerves,
and telling my children
it's what she deserves?

What am I worth,
what price can there be
for someone so useless?
I'm worthless, that's me.

God, you promise that not a sparrow should fall without your knowledge. Sometimes I feel smaller than a sparrow. As vulnerable as a frightened bird. I hide, I hide from the world, from people, from myself, even from you.

But you do not hide from me, God. You are there waiting to reach out to me, to lead me out of the dark places of my life. When I feel worthless you are my mirror, persuading me to look and see that, in your eyes, I am valued and loved.

Let me believe it.

Amen.

Fredwyn Hosier, England

No counsellors – please

This is the boy whose father
hanged himself at home.
He seems alone.

They feel he needs to speak
to tell them about his grief;
but he doesn't want to sit on soft chairs
while they tweezer out his tears.
There are parts of himself
that he wants to keep.

He doesn't want to talk of his trauma
or how he deals with his mother
but looks to school for relief;
the teacher who helps him write
and paint, makes him get on with maths,
the man who orders his life,

who lets him drop his dad into his day
as easy as putting sugar in his tea.

They want to tell him
bereavement is like a black hole
which shrinks in time,

but he doesn't want their words;
he's doing fine.

Denise Bennett, England

Empathy

Will you walk with me through the dark ways of life?
Be with me on the pathway,
fearfully, cautiously,
winding through unfamiliar times and places:
walk in my shoes – that you may accompany me on my journey?

But do not expect my shoes to be comfortable,
moulded as they are by my pounding feet.
Nooks and crannies corresponding to my idiosyncrasies
will not fit you.

Will you feel pinched, cramped, rubbed sore in my shoes?
Will you trip as overlarge shoes flap?
Can you take the discomfort of walking with me?
But will you come with me – come what may,
a Christ in disguise ministering to my need?

Ros Murphy, England

Someone's life

The heart breaks, the room falls silent, yet the piercing screams of the little girl inside get louder and louder, but no one moves a muscle, or maybe the screams can't be heard by the individual in today's society.

Does anyone really care?

The girl looks in the mirror trying to recall the happy memories in her life. Closing her bloodshot eyes the crystal glass breaks piece by piece and crumbles to the floor like the door of her tiny world closing behind her.

Grabbing a piece of freshly cut glass she directed it towards her wrist, where she knew soon enough her time would end. She cut her wrists one by one as if she was cutting food for a dinner party. Just as easy as ABC.

To her anyway!

Right then and there the girl's soul was covered in a poisoned shade of darkness. She closed the holy book of lies, denying to herself what she thought had happened. Which allowed her to drift off into a peaceful yet disturbing sleep.

Kayliegh Kirkham, England

God of the broken

God of the lonely,
hear me as I cry alone. Take my anger against those who laugh and deride
my sorrow; my frustration against those who belittle my pain; and my
despair of ever finding friendship. Take my feelings of futility and
misunderstanding, take my solitude and my yearnings for company, take
them all Lord, they are no use to me.

God of the bereaved,
touch me as I stifle a sob. Take the grief which threatens to overpower me; and
my bitterness at being left behind. Take my emptiness, my ache of despair; my
lack of joy, take them away Lord, they are no substitute for a life lost.

God of the betrayed,
see me as I struggle. Take my rage at those who turned against me and the
broken trust, shattered beyond repair. Take my impotence and feelings of
failure, take the wounds of destroyed hopes, take my retreat from the world
and longings to turn back the clock. Take them from me, Lord, ease the
burden of my guilt and helplessness.

Loving God,
creator of all,
redeemer of all,
sustainer of all,
take the shattered fragments of my life.
Through your love, mould them into a new creation,
designed for your purpose
and beautiful in your sight. Amen.

A. K. Heathcoat, England

A prayer for suffering love

Lord Jesus, as you accepted the cross, so may I embrace the way of
suffering love. Give me strength to learn how to meet the injustices of this
life with a love that draws me ever closer to others and to you. Amen.

Andrew Clitheroe, England

No place to go

(Written after a conversation with a homeless woman)

What do you want? I'd said. Well, for a start
I need a place to rest my heart.
Inside my head so many wars:
are you the one to open doors,
invite me in for family meals?
It's space I need, it's time that heals.
A home isn't where I hang my hat,
it's not a couch in someone's flat.
Don't want a handout or a loan,
I need a space to call my own.
Don't give me soup and good advice,
don't say it's free, I know the price.
Don't tell me what is right for me,
don't strip me of my dignity.
You want to help, you want to give,
so can you help me want to live?
She said, I'll talk, I like your face;
it's another day, another place.
I said, Yes, talk, for that's a start.
Let's find a place to rest your heart.

Lord, when I need a place to rest my heart I can always find it
in you. You know what it is to be in the wilderness and you walk
there with me. I go into the depths and you are there. No place
is so dark that I cannot find you.

There is often too much space in my life. Space in my thoughts
where fear and loneliness creep in and catch me unawares.
Space that haunts me and causes me to cry for it to be filled.

But, Lord, when I stop and look for that place to rest my heart, I
find I can talk to you. And that's the place to start. Amen.

Fredwyn Hosier, England

I have called you by your name and you are mine

(In memory of people who have died street-homeless)

God says, 'I have called you by your name and you are mine.'

God of love, call me by my name. Pronounce its syllable with care. Speak my full name, the name the world knows me by. Speak my private names, known only to my friends. My lovers, myself.

You know me from my beginning to my end. Speak my name and make me yours, for ever.

God says, 'Your name is engraved on the palm of my hand.'

God of infinite tenderness, who hurt your hand with my name? How did my name get cut into your palm? How did the blade wound your skin?

But when you curl your hand, my name is there, held in your powerful, gentle hand. Keep me safe, hold me tight, and let me never hurt you, or anyone again.

God says, 'I will give you a new name, known only to the one who receives it.'

God of power, you have the right to name me. You have known my character as it developed. You have seen my good times and been with me in my bad times. You know when I have spat and cursed and damaged those around me. You know when I have charmed and loved and helped to heal.

Let me come close to you, so that I can hear my name. You know the one that only you and I, only you and I, will ever know.

God says, 'I have called you by your name and you are mine.'

God of love, you speak the name of every person on earth. When we lean towards you, you speak our names and make us yours. When we turn to the world, we know the amazing truth that this same intimate love, this same total dignity, belongs to all the people we meet.

Give us the loving strength to honour every name and every person. Speak to us the names of the people we meet, remind us that you have called them by their names and all belong to you.

Janet Wootton. England

The cost of forgiveness

(A reflection for Holy Week following the murder of my 17-year-old niece)

The apostle Paul, Lord,
was a murderer, in a way.
He did not cast the first stone,
but he looked on and held
the coats for those who did;
and Stephen, a man of beauty,
integrity, and love, bled
and died before his eyes.
Yet Paul went on to become
one of God's greatest ambassadors,
through whom the Christian faith
spread far and wide.

More recently, Lord,
an unknown, solitary killer
picked up a stone
and battered a young girl,
full of life, and fun, and happiness
until she lay dead on the frozen earth
beside a church on New Year's Eve.
We do not know what will become
of this anonymous assassin,
but we remember this:
he is a fellow human being
for whom Christ bled and died.

With every stone that struck Stephen,
and every blow that battered Nicola,
the nails which tore your hands and feet,
dear Jesus, are hammered home.
And every Enniskillen or Dunblane,
where Cain still slaughters Abel,
you are crucified again,
and your anguished prayer
screams down the centuries
from the dawn of time:
'Father, forgive them;
they know not what they do.'

Carol Dixon, England

Our own Good Fridays

(On the anniversary of my niece Nicola's murder)

I never before imagined
    the pain God felt
as he saw his only son crucified.

I never before imagined
    the pain he feels
when any of his sons or daughters suffer.

I never before imagined
    the pain God felt
as he watched those who hammered home the nails,

or what he feels today
    for those who torture,
kill, or stand idly by in the face of agonizing injustice.

Loving, Father God
    who suffers with the oppressed
        and the oppressor,
    give us the strength to endure our own pain,
    and the grace to forgive those who hurt us,
    but above all, give us the courage and commitment
    to work for peace in our own lives and in our world.

Carol Dixon, England

Spirit, free in all the world

Spirit, free in all the world,
alive in the places some of us steer clear of:
dungeon
crack-house
refugee camp and prison;
enable us to look with open eyes and hearts and find your Spirit everywhere.
Amen.

Kate Gray, England

Hope

(James 2.14–26)

Clinging to the fragments of a tattered dream
she walks with head upright
bearing the colours of the flag –
black and blue –
of violence past and present
into the unfulfilled hope
of a new tomorrow
(pain-free).

For reflection
How do we bring hope to the abused?
What resources has God given to us to do so?
How do we say to victims that God desires a different tomorrow for you?
How do we help people to envisage a different future?
What will it cost?

Claire Smith, Guyana/USA

Free us to forgive ourselves

God, who loves traitor and terrorist, paedophile and pervert,
help us not to demonize others,
making monsters of them
and saints of ourselves,
lest we give up our integrity,
replacing it with self-righteousness,
seeing not the log in our own eye.

God, forgive us and free us to forgive ourselves.
We rejoice in your free grace. Amen.

Kate Gray, England

The school yard

The school yard,
tears raining down my face;
what can I do to make them stop?

Arguing, shouting, swearing,
every word punctuated by a curse,
every word stabs at my heart;
my head spins.

'Don't shout, Please don't shout.
Sorry, I didn't mean to do it.
Shout at me, it's my fault.
Stop arguing, stop shouting;
it's me, me, me.'

What have I done?
Why do they hate me?
Why don't they shout at me?

The bell rings,
it's time to go home.
Back to mummy and daddy,
back to the shouting.

Michael Watson, England

Special

There was always the chance
That I wouldn't be picked;
Standing there as the best friends
And the good at games were called,
Fear that I'd be left, not chosen, but
Taken because there was no one else.
The shame of it.

And later, a different game,
Where the hurts were deeper,
As groups paired into couples,
And I, not chosen or choosing,
Remained, the encouraging,
'Your turn next', ringing
Ever more hollow.

I'm a long time learning
How deeply I'm valued;
God-chosen and cherished
(Which doesn't deny the aloneness)
I'm set free to love in my turn.

Ann Lewin, England

Loneliness

Always alone
no one at home.

No one to talk to
no one to hold.

No friends but the TV
no guests but the videos.

Emptiness within
emptiness without
longing for love.

Silence
emptiness
a void.
No welcoming smile
no friendly word
Just a silent, empty void.

Meals for one
tickets for one
life for one
is agony.

The agony of decisions made alone
the agony of joys unshared
the agony of silent meals
the agony of memories
the agony of being alive.

Nobody there.
Nobody cares.

A.K. Heathcoat, England

The whole world will rejoice

We speak about compassion
With caring hearts of love
Yet still so many suffer
We cannot reach them all.
The loners and the bullies
The old folk lost in time,
The terrorist, the rapist
Convicted for such crime.

Still little children suffer
In many a war-torn land;
Homeless, the cold seek shelter
And we must lend a hand.
To end the wars, injustice,
'The whole world will rejoice'
When every tribe and nation
Share food with ample choice.

How hard it is to honour
The things we hold as true,
Yet all must stand together
Knowing what we must do.
Give water to the thirsting,
The hungry will be fed
The sick, the sad, the dying
Find comfort and a bed.

Oh fill us with compassion
To act the way we speak
When overcome by anger
To turn the other cheek.
Only when we recognize
Our brother, sister, friend
Share universal freedom,
The world rejoice again.

Tune: metre 7 6 7 6 D

Joan Heybourne, England

Bits of love

Between the busy traffic's flow,
across the counter and the till,
by gesture, look, by word and will,
like furnace sparks, they burn and glow.

With storm below and cloud above,
keen disappointment, bitter loss,
in spite of all there comes across
unlooked-for elements of love.

Just when we might expect it least,
a quiet voice, a note of calm
subdues the echoes of alarm
and inner tensions are released.

Not all is thoughtlessness and greed;
between the heartache and the pain
the spirit is not always vain,
and some resources meet the need.

Those bits of love which flash and flare
down winding corridors of dark
are like the altar lamps which mark
the way to hope out of despair.

They may be smothered, lost or missed,
but gold for ever will endure.
One thing at least we know for sure:
they never will cease to exist.

John Adamson Brown, England

Make your home among us

Christ, whom wood and nails could not contain,
let your life-giving spirit burst through
the walls of injustice.

Shatter the dullness of despair
with the colour of hope
and beckon us on as we dare to dream.

Transform the hearts of our oppressors
with the beat of compassion
that together we may shape the future.

Show us the horizon of promise
through the window of hope
that darkness gives way to light.

Easter God, make your home among us,
touch us with your resurrection spirit
and turn our silent smiles
into songs of joy.

Annabel Shilson-Thomas/CAFOD, England

God, you are a big God

A man from Wythenshawe, UK, in his mid-70s, who lived in Kenya for two years with the RAF, spoke about the time when he was invited to a young woman's initiation ceremony. He didn't say much except 'They were all right until we went in, these countries, saying we were trying to civilize them. We've done a lot of damage.'

God, you are a big God.
Bigger than armies and nations; bigger than our minds can fathom.
We don't often know what to think about what we have made of your world.
We want somehow to hope that things can be different and damage undone.
God,
when we are confused about what we have done to others,
bring us to awareness of our power to change life today.

Kate Gray, England

Cry of the child

Vulnerable God,
born in a stable,
born in the midst of poverty:
you come to set us free.

Crying for the millions
born too in slums,
born too in poverty:
we are set free by you.

Child from heaven,
free from disease
free from starvation
we cry to you . . .

We cry . . .
for babies born with HIV
for children made orphans by AIDS
for young people around the world with no medication
for families with no wage earners
for old people who become parents again
for people who are sick and dying . . .

Born in a stable,
born in the midst of poverty:
you come to set us free.
Living God, be with us all
and give us your freedom.

Martin Hazell, England

The Journey . . . Stations of the Cross . . .

(Accompanying a person living with AIDS from diagnosis to death)

This set of poems was written after seeing Penny Warden's 15 Stations of the Cross in Blackburn Cathedral, England.

In memory of Ronald.

1. Condemned

Now diagnosed
this is to be his last
last dance of life.

The steps disclosed
are those once
danced before –

the dance of death –
the last last dance
on earth's rough floor.

_____

2. Carries his cross

His mind and body
crossed
his spirit soars
beneath the weight
of such a load
with deepdown
inner strength
from him who trod
this way of gore
before.

3. First fall

Grappling with
frightening fears
he falls
fighting.
And fighting
finds his feet
again
on terra firma.

_____

4. His mother

She sees him through her tears.
She sees him streaming blue
beneath the darkening day.

That she so helpless
helplessly
should see him thus –

him whom she wombed
to life
not all that long ago.

5. Simon

He saw with seeing eyes
an image in disguise.
He saw the face of God.

And heard with ears to hear
a strangely plaintive plea:
Oh, love me. Love me.

And with languid arms
he lifted him, this load,
and helped him on the road.

_____

6. Veronica

Flushed
with the rush
of breath-breaking
anguish
from somewhere
alongside
she appears
to brush with her veil
and wash with her tears
the features she loved
and was now losing.

_____

7. Second fall

He falls.
Falling
retching
falling in his
wretchedness
feeling unloved
falling unloving –
he falls.

8. The Women

Wailing echoes through
the corridors of pain.
Weary washed-out
women wondering why
one so good, so young
should have to die.
And in his turmoil
gesturing peace
he passes by
his own peace failing.

_____

9. Third fall

Falling
falling
into the darkness
of bitter self-loathing
lost in unloving
he falls
towards dying
bereft even of his
selfless selfness.

_____

10. Stripped

Without resistance
he is stripped
by paid practitioners
who prod his nakedness.
Their dismal duty,
his deep forsakenness.

11. Nailed

Impassively
he lies outstretched
nailed to a cross-beamed
bed
nailed by clinical needles
bloodied by the last
of his blood
blue in the rays
of the draining day.

---

12. He dies

There is a sudden rush
of demi-semi-quavers
through his sore scored body
as he dies to the old music
battened to the bars
of his deathbed
not even noting the gravity
of the grave-clothes lying
in readiness.

---

13. Taken Down

Befriended by death
released and relaxed
gifted with peace
he is gently lifted
and softly lowered
by loving friends
reverencing his going.

14. The Tomb

Now,
where he lies
this gifted tomb
is walled with
angels' wings.

Its silence
that of waiting
waiting in the wings
before being partnered
for another dance.

---

15. Resurrection

He thought he'd danced
alone
that last last dance
the dance of death.
But now in resurrection
Son-light
he can see
my arms held his
upon his cross.
I was his longed-for
loving partner
in his earthly
last last dance.
But now new music sounds
where dancing is for ever.
Come! Dance! Arise!
Let's dance!

Harry Wiggett, South Africa

Rage's blood

Show us how to praise you, Lord,
even when life is black,
blackened by clouds of doubt.

Show us how to praise you, Lord,
even when life is grey,
greyed by grief's miseries.

Show us how to praise you, Lord,
even when life is colourless,
colourless by routine's sameness.

Show us how to praise you, Lord,
even when life is deepest red,
reddened by rage's outpoured blood.

Frances Ballantyne, England

First music

What stirrings these
within me as I feel
caressed by breezes
setting tremolos of rustling sounds
so gently homing
on my two sound-sensing drums
admitting them to where
my heart beats soundlessly
within?

First music
from that fruitful Eden tree –
music of the world
of God-created things
bringing me
through the listening
to a loving belonging
and a longing for
singing!

Harry Wiggett, South Africa

Thankfulness

Lord God, thank you for loving us,
for the gift of life and for the beauty of the world.
Thank you for those who love and support us
and for those we care for and love, too.
Thank you that when I forget or decide to ignore you,
walking away is not what you do.
So thank you for all the blessings you give,
for being beside me right now,
my Way, my Truth and my Life,
thanks be to you.

Andrew Clitheroe, England

A prayer for humility

Lord, unless you bless me
I shall not remain
in touch with this earth
into which you breathed
your destiny.

For this God-breathed 'me'
is no ordinary dust
but spirit and matter
fashioned to embrace
eternity.

Not just for me: for others too
when down to earth and in touch with heaven
we discover
death and resurrection
simultaneously.

Gathering precious dust
from all over the world
dear God of Divine story
make sense
of us.

Andrew Clitheroe, England

Advent dialogue

We are waiting for you
in the carol and manger,
in the glitter and tinsel,
sending cards 'With our love'.

> *I am waiting for you,*
> *born in squalor and danger,*
> *but, most risky and painful,*
> *I am waiting in love.*

We are looking for you
in the soul-stirring broadcast,
in the Oxfam tin rattle
and safe, distancing love.

> *I am waiting for you*
> *through the eyes of the outcast,*
> *in the ones who own nothing*
> *and in crucified love.*

Are we waiting for you
in the trumpet and glory
In the ending of time?
In the kingdom of Love?

> *I am waiting for you*
> *to respond to my story;*
> *live with all I have given*
> *in unending love.*

John Lansley, England

A prayer of service to others

Dear God of gentle love,
grant me a generous heart,
an open mind
and the vision
to see your image
in others. Amen.

Andrew Clitheroe, England

A prayer for forgiving love

Heavenly Father, as I follow in the footsteps of Jesus Christ, help me to find you in the darkness of the night that I might see you more clearly in the light of the day. And in forgiving love may I find the fulfilment of my life. Amen.

Andrew Clitheroe, England

Compassion

Suffering, sharing
The pain;
Knowing within oneself
Some of the cost.
Spurred to activity,
One hand stretched out
To those who suffer,
One stretched out to
God who suffers too.
Nothing sentimental:
The sharp edge of love,
Like crucifixion.

Ann Lewin, England

Send people who are compassionate

Send people who are passionate, O Lord,
to right what is unjust,
until your kingdom come.
Send people who are compassionate, O Lord,
to stand alongside those who are in pain,
until your will is done.
Send people who are humble, O Lord,
to make known the Good News,
until the world is won. Amen.

Peter Graystone, England

True love

True love,
that which is real,
knows no pretences.
It is bathed in tears
and shines
through life's absurdities.
It is not fazed
by laughter
nor by pain.
True love is not diluted or drowned
by words.
It will rest in a touch,
a look,

and say it all.

When you don't
know what to say or do,
it can just be.
It gathers up all our hopes
and rememberings and says,
'Let go into Me.'

True love never ends.

Jeanne Blowers, England

Moulded to compassion

I can understand and forgive
the lack of love so long ago.
But that does not
do away with the longing,
the needing to talk it out,
talk it through
in listening love.

I do not want you to say,
'I am sorry', or 'I pity you',
but just to hear and know.

To know
that holiday sun was not warmth
nor money real treasure.
Not to lack food
did not mean
I was not hungry,
starving to be fed
in so many ways.

A comfortable bed
did not give deep peace,
and stillness in the house
was all too often uneasy silence,
which did not make a quiet home.

Yet in all this,
I have come to see
that God used
the pain and suffering
that came my way,
to mould and fashion me,
to reduce me
to compassion.

Jeanne Blowers, England

81

Another world is possible

God, who smashes barriers
with storytelling and street theatre,
thank you,
that another world is possible!

God, seen in drag queen
with flamboyant colours and sequined dresses,
thank you,
that another world is possible!

God, living through our contradictions,
with contributions to creative new world dis/orders,
thank you,
that another world is possible!

Kate Gray, England

Dear God, you are our future

Dear God, you are our future
and we want to grow with you.

Dear God, you know the way we are heading
and we want to walk with you.

Dear God, sometimes we are worried
and we know we can talk with you.

Dear God, today we are hopeful
only because of you.

Dear God, we trust you
and place our future in your hands.

Vaughan Jones, England

Chapter Four

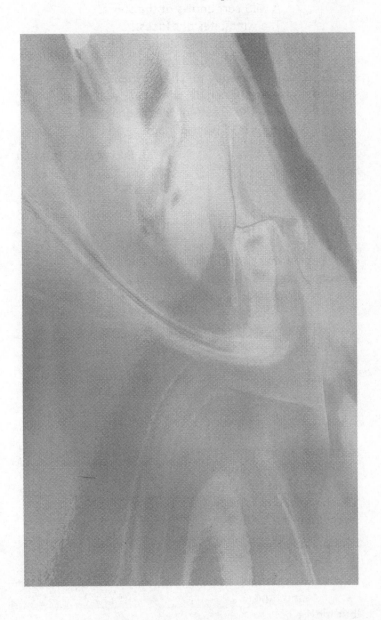

Creation - culture - community

moonlight

A wild surf gnaws at the shore.
The wind bites our faces.
Above, scattered clouds
slide swiftly, gold-graced.
In the gentle touch of a friend –
a hint of angels' wings.
And the breath of the moonlight
sighs a whisper of hope.

Robert Bos, Australia

Holding the pebble

That pebble was smooth, hard and cold,
    inanimate,
        unyielding,
            shaped by countless years of pounding seas and rocks.
Like millions more, it seemed –
yet not the same.
And as I held it in my hand,
exploring shape
    and size
        and texture,
            it changed –
absorbed my warmth,
darkened with moisture –
took something from me
which made a difference,
even if only for a while.

The world is hard
and shaped
    by circumstance
        and time,
but maybe
for a while,
even there,
I can make a difference.

Marjorie Dobson, England

King Country mist

King Country hills
shrouded in drifting mist.
Strong and still
ancient land
rising up
like God.
Mysterious
hiding,
peeking out.
Enticing us
to look, seek,
run into the soft folds
of God's being.
And rise up
with God
to bless the Light.

Wendy Ward,
Aotearoa New Zealand

Promise

There must have been a rainbow!

All the elements were there.
Blazing sun and sparkling water,
drops spinning in a wide arc
as water streamed from hair and
clothing,
rising from that river
after the blessing of baptism.

Everything else happened
to mirror the visions –
heaven opened,
the winged creature settled,
the voice spoke.
'My Son,
you please me.'

So, at this point of no return,
opening a promise
of new hope for all,

surely there must have been a
rainbow?

Marjorie Dobson, England

Creation Sunday

Lord God, Father of Creation,
you made all that exists from nothing:
spoke into existence each bird and tree,
designed the detail of each butterfly and flower,
made us from dust, one part of your world.

Lord God, Saviour of the world,
you made your covenant with all living creatures:
watch when a sparrow falls to the ground,
sustain all creation by your word,
send your Son to bring healing to creation.

Lord God, Spirit of life,
you breathe your image into human beings;
inspire us with love for your world,
charge us to care for all you have made,
invite us to steward and care for your world.

Blessed God, Father, Son, Spirit,
we praise you for all you have created.
Forgive us for taking your works for granted.
Equip us with vision and ability to fulfil our task:
to act justly, live simply and walk humbly with you, our God,
in the garden of your Creation.

Through Jesus Christ our Lord. Amen.

Dave Bookless, A Rocha UK, England

Rainsong

It falls in a veil,
the evening rain . . .
like wafting gauze,
diffusing all peripheries
between the see-er
and the seen;
it gentles free the clinging dust,
and coaxes into green
the faded grass –
upon whose glistening spears
it hangs and gleams
like jewels upon a skein . . .
soft fall and welcome
mantle over all embraced
in misting drift –
to blend the vespered edge
of brief dark's swift
encroach and crystallize
through vapour furled
the cool uncurling
of the coming night.
So may the hours
restore the thirsty earth
with distillation sweet . . .
until the early light
rejects in tatters grey
retreating clouds,
and pinks the fresh perfection
of the infant day
in opal shrouds of gossamer.

Margot Arthurton, England

Prayer of commitment

For the sake of the earth, for our
children's sake, for God's sake.

Oceans warming
Coral dying
Sea rising
Land disappearing
Ice caps melting
Polar bears dying
Rivers flooding
Waters overwhelming.
All: Calming, caring God . . .
Help us act to still the storm
For now, for ever.

Storms destroying
Chaos reigning
Cities flooding
People moving
Disease spreading
Homes disappearing
Crops failing
Hope fading.
All: Calming, caring God . . .
Help us act to still the storm
For now, for ever.

Planet shaping
World creating
Life forming
Spirit breathing
Law guiding
Cradle birthing
Cross bearing
Hope rising.
All: Calming, caring God . . .
Help us act to still the storm
For now, for ever.

Christian Ecology Link, England

Rainforest (1)

One more tree
thwacks against its neighbour in domino progression.
A ferocious whispering of clashing leaves
as the canopy is torn away.
Its occupants, exposed, fly shrieking to the sky.
And from the undergrowth,
now withering and smashed,
a scampering and slithering.

With each splintering crack and crash
the earth judders into barrenness.
From this once bounteous dwelling place
its human populace slink into unforgiving cities,
discover poverty, are introduced to fear.
Hunger-driven, they survive knee-deep in trash.
Life trickles into mere existence
as sun-scorched clouds evaporate
above an earth sucked dry by greed.

Just one more tree.

Christine Ractliff, England

Rainforest (2)

Look up from your way with words.

Watch how each day I inhale the sun,
send my sap foraging for lush pigments,
my vivid streaks to dart as daylight
across my forest floor.

Have you heard me

swinging arcs of rainbow between branches,
flapping swarms of light through a weave of trees,
drumming my rhythm on the skin of pools,
flicking a blaze of neon wings to rise,
shrieking riot of colour up as air?

For you, world
every day this fusion of life is my prayer.

Eve Jackson, England

Spring

Stand silently and see at winter's edge
small subtle signs of spring emerge once more . . .
The sparkling drop of fretted frost in thaw
fractures puddles, softening stone of earth;
brittle twigs bud-bursting from the dark,
and glorious madder-hue of willow bark.

See sparrows, feather smooth,
abandon winter's ruff,
and fish, who view the rippled sky
through limpid eye,
released from bitter cast iron cave
by shy sweet warmth of midday sun
hung briefly, damply, out to dry.

See crocus spears emerge –
protecting pregnant buds which staunchly grow
beneath the still-chill legacy of wind –
and early gold of aconite
in shining contrast to the lingering snow.
Stand silently and see in everything
small potent portents of the Spring –
gaze, wondering, at the life they bring
from winter's death.

And sing!

Margot Arthurton, England

The Operation Noah prayer

Creator God, how deep are your designs!
You made a living earth, cloud, rain and wind,
and charged us with their care.

We confess that the way we live today
is changing the climate, the seas and the balance of life,
dispossessing the poor and future generations.

Build our lives into an Ark for all creation,
and, as you promised Noah never to repeat the Flood,
so makes us heralds of a new rainbow covenant:
choosing life for all that is at risk –
for creation, neighbours near and far,
our children and ourselves. Amen.

Christian Ecology Link

Our world

Planes soar
cars roar
people snore.
Blinded by ignorance!
Influenced by power!

Our world is crumbling beneath our feet.

Lies, lies, lies and more.
Governments barely spare a passing glance,
hiding behind their power feeling safe and secure!

Our world once flourished green, blue and all!
Now in the petrol fumes our world is grey with ignorance!

Our once beautiful world . . .
. . . is now dying!

Martin Edwards, aged 10, England

Rediscovering the rainbow

Look up at the sky.
Watch the easy jets go by.
Their vapour trails concealing
toxic damage to the ceiling
of our amazing Earth.
No one asking, 'Is this journey worth
the cost that sets the climate reeling?'

Smell the car-polluted haze
of the complicated maze
of motorways and urban sprawl,
snarling, queuing, at a crawl,
asthmatic mark of prowess.
But at what price this progress,
when pride precedes a fall?

See the power stations' plume
that shadows all in gloom,
slowly suffocating pillow
from a never-ending billow
that masks the clear blue sky.
But no one's asking why
the climate's going awry down below.

Are we blocking without trace
the spectrum-filled embrace
of God's promise for creation?
It's time to stop this aberration,
to reduce, recycle, reuse,
to review and not abuse
God's gifts. Earth needs our consideration.

It's time to rediscover . . .
the rainbow.

Marie Birkinshaw, England

Birds

Flying in the sky.
Infinite numbers of starlings
rise over similar quantities of children.
Two different species of animal;
one standing,
one soaring.

Hannah Warwicker, England

Kiss of life

I saw the moon's eclipse last night –
rose-veiled intrusion in between
the lambent burning fiery glow
and ice-cool satin sheen

I saw a comet, hanging bright,
low down upon the velvet dark . . .
The air stood cool and quiet – and still
raw daylight, quite concealed within
the deep horizon's quick,
lay – sleeping . . . promised.

Then in the clear of wakening dawn
I saw the touch of dew –
the crystal shine on shadowed lawn
awaiting longed-for sun's release,
and morning born anew.

I saw the warmth of afternoon,
I heard the mower's song –
the sweet-green smell of fresh-cut sap
bled soft upon the air . . .

It was the kiss of summer's youth,
it was a lover's kiss –
if this should be the kiss of life,

then life is bliss!

Margot Arthurton, England

Take a walk on the wild side

Can you spot the hidden animal?

Take a walk on the wild side
Step forward, open your eyes wide
Where the mighty stag **B**ellows
Hedgehogs rustle the floor
The mouse cowers in d**A**rkness
Watching great eagle soar
Where the re**D** squirrel darts
And the pine martens play
In this world far away
From your tree fellin**G** day
Dream of great bears roaming here
Proud, mighty, strong fierc**E**
The wolf loping and howling
Teeth ready to pie**R**ce
But you'll be back tomorrow
In your big JCB
Just keep your eyes open
And who knows what you'll see?

Hannah Warwicker, England

The water meter

I have a water meter,
it's underneath the stairs.
I'll show you how that meter
helps me to say my prayers.

I pray I will be able
to pay my bills on time.
I pray I will not have to
resort to fraud or crime.

I pray I will still manage
to wash and clean and such.
I pray that all my children
don't have to suffer much.

I pray I will not have to
cut down on vital things,
like washing up or showers
in which my husband sings.

I pray that global warming
won't bring floods down our way.
I pray there's enough water
to run my tap each day.

I have a water meter,
it's underneath the stairs.
I know that water meter
has helped me say my prayers.

Metre 7 6 7 6 if sung as six verses
or 7 6 7 6 D if sung as three verses.

Janet Lees, England

93

I am

I am the protective ozone layer
of the Earth community.
I filter the sun's rays so that life is possible.
Yet over recent decades a wound
has appeared in my side, a deep gash
that now endangers my very existence.

I am the invisible air that supports life
for both creatures and plants.
Yet I cry in pain because of the pollutants,
the acids, the oxides, the heavy metals
and the particular matter that is pumped into me,
choking me and choking all of life.

I am the water of life that flows
in the seas, rivers, blood streams and sap.
No life is possible without my presence and flow.
Yet I am forced to carry poisons
that kill those that depend upon me.
I am treated as a sewer.

I was the Larsen B ice-shelf.
I speak with sadness as recently I collapsed
sending 720 billion tonnes of ice into the sea
to drift and slowly melt. I am no longer.
I forced the sea to rise threatening
coral islands and lowlands all over the Earth.

I am the Sahara.
I am the great desert of sand creeping south,
smothering the valuable land on which
millions of Earth creatures rely.
I am growing yet this is at the cost of life
and of opportunities for life.

I am the luscious rainforest of the Amazon.
I hold and care for an amazing variety
of species, both flora and fauna.
I am the Earth community's lung taking in
carbon dioxide and producing necessary oxygen.
Yet I am rapidly shrinking. My timber is being pillaged
and I cry for future generations.

94

I am the fertile land that is tired and threatened.
I struggle to provide food for ungrateful humans
who continue to dig holes in me, to shower me
with industrial fertilizer and to push me to my limits.
How can I continue to stay well
while contributing to my Earth community?

I am the indigenous person,
the one who is the land,
the tangata whenua of each and every place.
I am whole when the land is whole.
My spirit soars when the spirit of the land soars.
Yet I have been violated, my spirit has been broken.
The land has been taken and ravaged and
I have been colonized and pushed to the margins.

I am the poor person
who lives both on the land and in the city slums.
I crave for enough food
and my spirit cries out for the opportunity to live.
I dream of a day when no one will be hungry,
when no one will be homeless. When will this be?

I am Jesus, the One who says I am.

David Tutty, Aotearoa New Zealand

A prayer about fresh air

God
I heard a poor man saying
I have not enough to buy
fresh air
land speculators determine
that too
I suddenly realized.
Would we not meet you
in nature
forgive me if I ask.

Basil Fernando, Sri Lanka

Hopes of youth

From young offender to reptile keeper
Nathan is 15 years old and from South London:

I got done for taking a car,
It's a gang thing.
If a stranger came round here
he'd get beaten up.
But I got an A in my essay.
I was proud.
I like snakes.
I've got my own snake.
I'd like to be a reptile keeper in a zoo.

From child soldier to mechanic
Zaduma is 15 years old and from the Democratic Republic of the Congo:

I was abducted from my village.
I was given a gun and told to fight.
I killed at least two people.
I asked God to forgive me.
I ran away.
I was afraid they would catch me.
I wanted to go back to my village
to go to school and play football.
I want to be a mechanic.

(add more global stories known to you)

Jesus of Nazareth,
You grew up in an occupied country.
You learnt a trade.
You had hopes.
Help us to nurture the hopes of young people,
that lost opportunities may be made up,
and dreams may become reality.

Janet Lees, England

Amazing Lord

Lord, how amazing is your power!
You have created this earth and all its peoples,
blessed them with gifts both great and small –
yet still sometimes your children cannot see you.

**Open our eyes, Lord, that we may see your glory in the beauty of
the earth and in the countless talents of its people.**

Lord, how spectacular are your ways!
You have walked across rough water, stilled a storm,
healed the sick, raised Lazarus from the tomb –
yet still sometimes your children cannot hear you.

**Open our ears, Lord, that we may hear your word and pass it on to
others, that all may follow your guiding call.**

Lord, how mysterious is your presence!
We cannot see your face, your stature is beyond imagining.
Nor can we estimate how infinite your love –
yet still sometimes your children cannot find you.

**Open our hearts, Lord,
so we may forgive as you forgive us,
so we may heal as you heal us,
so we may share as you share with us,
so we may love as you love us.**

Christine Ractliff, England

Desert blessing

God of the refreshing whisper of a dawn breeze:
Whisper your blessings upon us.

God of the unrelenting heat of the desert sun:
Strengthen us with your blessings.

God of the furious raging sand storm:
Shelter us with your blessings.

God of the rhythmic dancing firelight:
May we share your blessings with one another.

Clare McBeath, England

...arated from Mother Earth

Mother Earth, how appropriate to call you so
for you indeed nourish our lives like a mother.
You sustain us with food,
and provide us with shelter.
You freely give us lots of things to enjoy.

But we have abused our freedom to enjoy your gifts to us.
We have cleared your forests and flattened your mountains
to create giant buildings and hard structures that we think will last and edify us.
We have dirtied your waters and air with wastes and toxic matters
and choked your throat and lungs with non-biodegradable stuff
to enjoy the ease of travel and the fruits of our human inventions.
We have covered you with concrete to free ourselves
from the dust that reminds us we all came from you.
We have even hoarded your goods for ourselves
without thinking of the needs of others.

We have not raised our children as your own
so they know you only as dirt and soil, but not as Mother Earth.
Our advances in science have made us too fearful of things
    squiggly and squirmy
so we have taught our children that you are filthy,
just something to step on
just something to spit on.

Mother Earth, what has gone awry that we have become separated from you?
Is it the thought that matter does not matter as much as the spirit?
Is it the belief that God, being greater, beyond and above matter,
    is also apart from matter?
Is it the belief that we human beings are the 'crowning glory of creation',
free to do anything we like with anything in creation?

Mother Earth, we need to be in touch with you again.
We need to realize that matter and spirit do matter together,
and that God's own spirit hovers over your whole being.
We need to see God's image not only in human beings
but also in you as God's very own handiwork of love.
We need to remember that our blessings from God
to thrive and flourish are tied with the need for us to care for you.

Hope S. Antone, Asian Women's Resource Centre for Culture
and Theology and other women's groups, Malaysia

Creation, culture, community

God of creation
Spring turns to summer
Leaves burst forth
The rain falls upon the earth
The moon tugs the tidal seas
Day follows night and night follows day
Mountains look down from their lofty heights
Forests inhale deeply cleaning the air
A majestic confidence breathed through creation.

God of our urban culture
Dandelions break through concrete, proclaiming your glory
Birds sing in back yards, building nests for the next generation
Café umbrellas flutter in the warm breeze
Glasses chink to the sound of gentle laughter
Skyscrapers shoot their way confidently into the sky
Steel windmill sculptures celebrate industrial heritage
Street entertainers croon familiar songs of lovers
A bustling confidence of urban culture.

God of our diverse community
A toddler takes her first faltering steps
An elderly woman sits regally on a bench enjoying the view
A young man questions his sexuality
A couple begin to decorate their first home together
A grandmother takes grandchildren to the museum
A woman becomes an apprentice and steps inside the university
A man sits in the park with his dog, basking in the glory of spring
A quiet confidence seeping through community.

God of creation
God of our urban culture
God of our community
breathe through us your quiet assurance
breathe through us your steadfast love
breathe through us your gentle confidence
That we may be all you aspire us to be.

Clare McBeath, England

Ecological and economic justice

(A prayer of confession)

God our Mother, God our Father,
you, whom we have experienced and continue to
experience as Creator, Christ and Comforter,
hear us your children as we bring to you our
prayers for ecological and economic justice.

In awe and splendour we marvel at the work of
your hands with creation.
Only a God who is creative and imaginative could
create such beauty for our eyes to behold:
the Caribbean Sea that forms the backdrop for
our mountains, hills, plateaus and valleys;
our rivers, streams and springs that flow with life,
reminding us of your faithfulness and everlasting
love for humanity.

And yet, we have failed to be good caretakers
of your providence, even as we sing praises in
honour of creation.
We have failed to nurture, to protect and to
preserve Mother Earth and her bounties.
We have taken for granted that creation embodies
your love, presence and grace among us.
Have mercy upon us,
Jehovah Hoseenu (God our Maker).

We have plundered, wasted and misappropriated
your economic gifts.
Many are suffering at our hands because we have
allowed our greed, our envy and our selfishness
to stand in the way of equality, justice and
responsibilities for our communities.
We have abandoned the needs of our children,
sisters and brothers so as to create our own
'kingdoms of power' at the expense of perpetual
poverty and depravity.

**Gracious God, have mercy upon us. Forgive us,
Jehovah Jireh (God our Provider).
Cause us to recognize and to understand that
in creating you created for the needs of your
people, therefore, no one should lack or want
anything.**

Turn us aright.
Stir our consciences and awaken our
consciousness.
Stir our hearts, our will, and our desires that they
may be illuminated and ignited by the fire of your
love.
Renew us by the power of the Holy Spirit
dwelling in our lives so that together we may
all have life and have it more abundantly. Amen.

Tara Tyme, Jamaica and the Cayman Islands

A prayer of thanksgiving for creation and communion:

Inspiring God, we thank you for the earth and the waters, for the sky, air
and moon tonight, for the living creatures who make this earth their home.
We praise you for the gift of life, so we are born afresh each day.
We praise you for the gift of life and so we turn to Christ who is the
salvation of the universe.
Christ, you are made known to us in this Bread of Life.

Inspiring God, we thank you for our homes, relationships and patterns of
daily living, for your peoples who inhabit the earth and make it their home,
for peoples far and near all around the earth, your creation.
We praise you for renewing and regenerating the earth, so it can be born
afresh throughout generations.
We praise you for the gift of the earth and so we turn to Christ who is the
salvation of the universe.
Christ, you are made known to us in this Cup of Healing.

Kate Gray, England

A prayer from the Pacific

God Almighty, Creator and Sustainer,
it is you, Lord, who created our lands,
resources and our cultures which we enjoyed.
You expected us to use them
according to your will.
Our freedom has led us astray
to damage our cultures and environments;
we have neglected the obligation
to look after our lands.

Merciful God, we confess all our wrongdoings,
particularly those
that have affected our lands and ourselves.
For the climate change,
which has resulted in the sea level rise;
for the pandemic HIV/AIDS
which has killed our people;
for the economic globalization
which has ruined our cultures,
and the new culture
which has torn our families apart
and left many in poverty and depressed.

Merciful God,
we bring all these worries into your presence.
We beseech you
to awaken the eyes of those responsible.
Empower us,
with all the children of God across the globe
to continue to pray and work for peace and justice.
Strengthen our faith in you, our Triune God,
give us hope in Jesus as the sign of all times.
In his name we pray. Amen.

Rotaiti Kabatiiaa, Tarawa, Republic of Kiribati

Reckless living – prodigal moments

An old heaven and an old earth
Storms and wrecked lives
Floods and weeping
Drought and starvation
Unfair trade and worn-out hands
Rich and poor
Disease and heartache
Greed and suffering
Spiritual famine.

**in between –
some
prodigal
moments**
where the recklessness of human living

remembers
and
returns
to the
recklessness
of God's
love

A new heaven and a new earth
Seasons and joy
Still waters and green pastures
Rain and refreshment
Fair trade and good work
Enough for all
Health and healing
Care and well-being
Spiritual feast.

David Pickering, England

We celebrate the creation

Silence

The sound of a rain stick

Leader 1: God looked into emptiness and created all that is.
God spread out the earth in all its diversity,
with mountains and valleys, rivers and fertile plains.
There were patches of flood and fire,
of dryness and vivid green,
embraced by wind and sea –
a sun-filled landscape of hospitality.

*(A green cloth is spread and seeds,
flowers and fruits are placed on it;
a blue cloth is placed down like a flowing stream.)*

Leader 2: And, threading through it all,
like weavings of fervent hope,
were dreams of justice and compassion
and gentle streams of peace.

*(Purple threads are placed on the green cloth
and among the seeds, flowers and fruit.)*

Leader 1: God gathered all people into community,
gave a sigh of joy and set us free
to choose our path in a daring adventure of trust.

**Together: This is our God.
This is the wonder of our calling in faith.
Let us worship God.**

Song: (stand) Hallelujah! Hallelujah! Hallelujah! Hallelujah! (x3)

The creation groans

Leader 1: As we come together across the world
and stand before the Holy God
the voices of the people rise in lament and confession.

*(Those who will voice out laments and confession
will come to the blue cloth and touch it.)*

**Voices: We weep, O God, for the lives of our people.
We weep for the lives of women and children.**

1. We toil day and night and still our children go hungry.
2. We sow the fields but all that is left are the crumbs from the tables of the rich.
3. We leave our families to serve as migrant workers in cities and foreign lands.

Violence desecrates us and the earth.
We fall back in life without education and freedom.
We die from lack of health care.

4. We bow our heads in shame, O God,
for our tables groan with plenty.
Our only questions are about which good things to eat,
and how much is too much.
As we hear the cries of the suffering people in the distance,
we know that we have betrayed your dream.
We have failed to live in your just community.
And there are structures and systems in our world
that keep us in a divided world.

A silence is kept.

Leader: Lord, have mercy.
All: **Christ, have mercy.**

A silence is kept.

The coming of the Word

Leader: Nothing in all creation can separate us
from the love of Christ Jesus.
God hears the cries of the people
and gathers them into arms of love and justice.
Those who come in repentance and faith
are forgiven and invited to be part
of the restoration of the reign of God.

The sound of the rain stick

The Scripture

'Let justice roll down like waters and
righteousness like an ever-flowing stream' (Amos 5.24)

(Four women say the text repeatedly while waving the blue cloth like a river.)

Prayer*

Dear God,
we share the groaning, weeping and lamenting
not only of your people but also of your whole creation.
It is for this that we gather here.
We await your coming
as the source and embodiment of love and justice.
In the face of powers and principalities that cause
violence, injustice and un-peace in our time,
we pray again and again for your justice to roll down as waters
and your righteousness as an ever-flowing stream.
May it touch leaders and governments that they
may hear the cries of the suffering peoples.
May it transform structures so there will be
life-promoting and just trade for all.
May it change our lives – so that we become
strengthened by your spirit,
inspired by your compassion,
empowered by your will
to make all things new in your reign of
love, justice and peace for all.*

(The women put the cloth down after the prayer.)

Song of dedication – God of justice, God of mercy

(While the song is sung, the purple threads are gathered from the cloth and are distributed.)

God of justice, God of mercy, make us merciful and just!
Help us see all your creation as from you a sacred trust.
And when people cry in anguish for their own or others' pain,
Show us ways to make a difference, O dear God, make us humane!

How can we, as people chosen by your grace for service here,
How endure another's hardship without offering hope and cheer?
God, forgive us, we beseech you when our love fails to empower,
Teach us how to be more faithful in this present, crucial hour.

You have formed us, God of rainbows, in your image for your will,
Seeing our diverse reflections trusting you, we marvel still:
For our colours, strengths and talents show what one alone would lack,
Calling us to work together, brown, red, golden, white and black.

106

Grant all people work with meaning, strength to care for those they love,
Food for table, truth for telling, challenges to rise above.
But remind us, God of justice, this is now our work, our call!
Changing life's oppressive systems into ones empowering all.

So the vision you have planted in each human mind and heart
Now becomes the spark of action calling us to do our part.
Keep that vision clear before us: men and women, girls and boys
Valued in response and witness, sharing challenges and joys.

Blessing (through action)

Leader: Turn to a partner and tie the thread around her/his wrist,
            while sharing your commitment, and give each other a blessing.

Prayer prepared by Hope S. Antone
Liturgy prepared by Corazon Tabing-Reyes, Christian Conference of Asia

Respecting the earth and its people

(From CAFOD's Unearth Justice Campaign, which is calling for a
fairer distribution of the world's natural resources)

Creator God,
in your hands you hold the depths of the earth
and the heights of the mountains,
for all creation belongs to you.
Grant us grace to cherish your world
and wisdom to nurture its resources.
Save us from the desire to control what is not ours
and the impulse to possess what is there to share.
Give us insight to see where power is abused
and courage to speak out where truth is negated.
Guard us against complacency in the face of arrogant destruction
and ignite us with holy rage where fires of conflict are fanned by greed.
Forge in us hearts of gold to meet suffering with compassion
and wills of iron to challenge injustice with purpose.
Inspire us ever to search your ways and find new paths
that we may join hands with friend and stranger
to unearth justice and find lasting treasure. Amen.

Annabel Shilson-Thomas/CAFOD, England

The Spirit gives us ears

(A litany)

This is a statement to be shared among different voices and with music that is sympathetic to the mood and meaning of the statement. With some imagination it might be possible to convey dramatically or symbolically the situations described in this litany.

Listen
The Spirit gives us ears
Hear the voices
A mother crying for her lifeless child
A wife moaning after another beating
A child begging and people are passing
Doctors giving more bad news in clinics
Market traders calling selling
For less than it cost to grow
Board meetings celebrating profit updates
Politicians doing deals, pocketing bribes
Prayers and whisperings
As the time of detonation nears

Quiet

Listen
The Spirit gives us ears
Hear the sound
Footsteps dragging
Carrying water, collecting firewood
Dumping the body of a trade unionist
In a lonely spot
Trees crashing and logging lorries idling
The quiet ooze of factory waste
Sewing machines humming, stock crashing
Landmines clicking
Bombs bursting
Earth shattering

Listen
Hear the Spirit's voice
Hear her weep

Music

Listen
The Spirit gives us ears
Hear the voices
Hear the sounds
Campaigners challenging
Protesters demonstrating
Workers negotiating
Governments conceding
Corporations accounting
Men confessing
People changing
Earth sighing

Listen
Hear the Spirit's voice
Hear her sing

Music

Life Giving Spirit
Invite us again to
Treat the earth gently and each other justly
Bind us together
To work for justice
In the economy and the earth
Seal us in a Covenant
That gives dignity to us all
Men and women
Young and old
Black and white
Seal us in a Covenant
That anoints the wounded
Humbles the proud
And resists evil without doing harm
Seal us in a Covenant
That cherishes the earth
Challenges injustice
And chooses life
Life in fullness
Life revealed
Empowered and exalted
By the coming of Christ

World Alliance of Reformed Churches, Switzerland

Spirit of the living God

Spirit of the living God,
Creator of lively living,
fill us with thanksgiving
for the fact that we are here.

Spirit of the living God,
Comforter for people
who find life difficult today,
give us the words – or the silence –
to empathize where there is sadness.
Forgive us when we cause hurt
and create a lack of confidence
for a precious individual.

Spirit of the living God,
Motivator of the servant church
give us the spiritual power,
the resources, the desire,
to embrace the needs of our community,
to see things as they are in reality,
to forgive the unlovely things around us,
to take on board the need for redemption,
to listen to each other
and go where the Spirit leads. Amen.

Geoffrey Duncan, England

Chapter Five

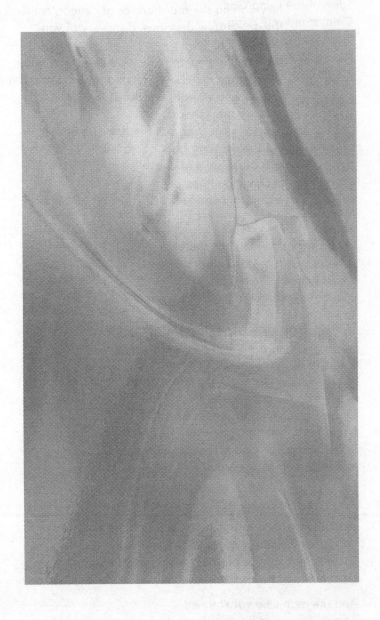

Moments of grace

Presence

Never mind the murmurings of delight, rather it was wham!
the delectable, delicious, discovery of you,
the shock of you
the smell of you on me – clothes, skin, tongue.
Which took me elsewhere and brought me to myself.
That is who you are and what you did.
That was the shock.
I wasn't expecting it – the drawing of you,
like the drawing back of waves
into the middle of a lake
beckoning almost,
without any words.
Presence.

Kate Gray, England

In the light of a new morning

The light of the morning for one man
remains buried beneath the trauma of that single moment
which aborted the ordinary, smothered the colour of his world,
blurred meaning, hid sense beneath a choke of grief
rising from hostility. His belief – his certainty – evaporating
in a sky-blue-ugly space that appeared
in a blink and blink again of an eye.

Another man
collected his shattered pieces,
matched them to something vaster, more meaningful
than grainy pictures of his life and set out,
knowing the light of morning was to be found
on some road he had still to walk.

And the man who sat stunned,
unmoving, raised his eyes from the ruined pages of his past
and glimpsed the sun – at last – scribbling his name.
A simple gesture that made him smile.

Eve Jackson, England

Compassionate God

Compassionate God,
come to us,
reveal yourself to us,
open your arms to us,
circle us with your embrace,
open your heart to us,
warm us with your love,
open your mind to us,
teach us with your knowledge,
come to us,
compassionate God.

Frances Ballantyne, England

Rainbow spirit

Rainbow spirit
rainbow spirit
you are knitting heaven and earth.
Rainbow spirit
rainbow spirit
you are painting fresh new life.
Rainbow spirit
rainbow spirit
you are pouring out new colour.
We with you are rainbow people! Amen.

Kate Gray, England

A prayer of a desperate parent

God of quiet and serenity,
grant me patience as I tend to the morning chores
and the baby is screaming.
Encircle me with your calm as I try to concentrate on written work
and the baby is screaming.
Enfold me in your peace as I continue on the daily round
and the baby is screaming.

Zam Walker, Wales/Scotland

receive me

a slow mounding of water
to a momentary peak
before tumbling gleefully forward
in a quick rush of foam to the beach
where it seeks out rocky crevasses
and swirls serenely
while slowly dissolving back
into its ancestral salty vastness
its life work accomplished

when my life's purpose is run
in your good time
Life-breather
Life-receiver
melt me back into you
and your beloved creation

Robert Bos, Australia

Lily is born

She is passed from cradle to cradle
of grandparents' arms,
floating in her warm curl of sleep,
slowly flowering as the minutes on the hospital clock
move her closer, closer to realizing she is born.

We too need time,
gathering with love to give,
to measure her future,
to catch our ageing selves
in her new-born breaths.

We counted stars all the way home.
It was late as we stood, listening,
inhaling happiness in the dark of the garden,
imagining where flowers
were blossoming.

Eve Jackson, England

Silence together

We hold silence together,
we make silence together,
we play and dance around it and then in it.
We go right into its midst.
We are cupping it in our hands – yours and mine.
We could smash it with dull words,
damage its sincerity with an, almost, palatable version and yet,
we do not want any less than excellence together . . .
Created, moulded, held, danced, feasted on.
Silence together.

Kate Gray, England

Spice trade

The small blue pottery jars on the pantry shelf
hold peppercorns, cloves, nutmegs, cinnamon quills,
cardamom pods and powdery ginger. Dull and drab.
But ease the corks and breathe the sensuous scent of history.

More precious than jewels a handful of pepper
smuggled from the East for Europe's queens and kings.
Cloves against plague, cinnamon to mask decay,
nutmeg for visions of flying, and ginger for gilded cakes.

For these, oceans were claimed and conquered
and adventurers sailed beyond the world's edge
to seize the spicy prize and trade for gold,
and sell the people of the fragrant groves.

Empires, enterprises, corporations and cartels
have sprouted from the spicy-island seeds
to weave their tendrils in a strangling net of trade
that traps struggling captives in a mesh of poverty.

A fortune of bittersweet spices scented the crucified body.
The risen Jesus shed the linen shroud and spice,
and unencumbered walked out into the morning
to share his life and freedom and break all bonds.

Diana Roberts, Aotearoa New Zealand

A moment of grace

I saw a policeman this morning,
standing on the pavement,
taking notes as he looked down
on a man.
White frizzy beard, no moustache,
clad like the half naked fakir.
Dead.

Sixty? Seventy? More years than I.
How did they go?
Were there better days,
or was it a slow decline into nothingness?
Did he ever dream the end would come like this,
alone,
on a dirty pavement?

A body in a hospital morgue,
unclaimed,
heart, lungs, kidneys, brain,
dissected to reveal their secrets,
but not his name,
his pain.

He made one final statement though,
lying there on the doorstep of a Parsee fire temple,
a Muslim, adorned with the golden marigold,
symbol too of Hindu reverence,
moving on, the many paths becoming one
before the One.

Astrid Lobo Gajiwala, India

Mary meets Buddha's mother

'You are Mary, I know,'
she said.
'I know you too,'
said Mary.

In front walked
a procession of women.
They were going
in search of their children;
the disappeared, the wounded,
    the tortured.

'You have seen all that,'
said the Buddha's mother.
'So have you too,
hearing from your son,' said Mary.

Silently they moved
behind the procession.
The crowd increased,
the journey was never-ending.
Two mothers followed,
never thinking of deserting.

Basil Fernando, Sri Lanka

Final suppers

I eat the bread
The meal is set
I drink the wine.

The loaf is plentiful
I give and receive
I eat the bread.

It is passionately red
Bitter as betrayal
I drink the wine.

Prayer is uttered
Everyone is fed
I eat the bread.

Everyone is offered
None refuse
I drink the wine.

All are forgiven
None are abandoned
We eat the bread
We drink the wine.

Mandla Gobledale, USA/Australia

117

Freeing God

'If your child were to state:
"I want to become a Buddhist,"
what would you say?'

I answered an unqualified 'Yes.'

I felt his shock, his pain.
Good, Catholic mother,
how could I betray
the faith of my fathers?
Had I not been fed on the one and only,
The Way, *The* Truth and *The* Life?

Perhaps my response should have been less stark,
but it seemed at that moment
that the question was a test
and the answer had but one meaning:
for or against the Christ.

And yet, dear Bishop,
my 'Yes' was, so to speak,
only the tip of the iceberg,
for I began asking myself your question
long ago, at different points in time.

In the path that I have chosen[1]
where God has many names
and religions are but doorways to the Beyond,
it is an inevitable introspection,
marking a turning point,
a challenge, if you will,
to give truth to one's belief,
to let go unconditionally
in the God the name evokes.

The Ultimate, the Absolute, the Supreme,
The Ground of Our Being,
Abba, Christ, Ruah.
Brahma, Vishnu, Mahesh,[2]
Yahweh, Allah, Enlightened One,
Sophia, Saraswati,[3] *Shakti,*[4]
Mahalaxmi,[5] *Maheshwari,*[6] *Mahakali,*[7]
Ma.[8]

Striking the human breast,
they awaken within
a consciousness
of the Human and the Divine;
our creation, our legacy, our life,
immanent, transcendent.

Does it matter then,
who strikes the door,
or more,
that we hear the knock
and step across the threshold
into that Space that beckons all,
to cry out, to listen,
to struggle, to share,
to bleed, to heal,
to weep, to comfort,
to be destroyed, to rise,
together,
as one,
Human,
Divine.

Astrid Lobo Gajiwala, India

1 I am a Catholic married to a Hindu and we have three children with dual religious identities.
2 The Hindu male Trinity: the Creator, the Sustainer, the Destroyer.
3 Hindu Goddess of Knowledge, religious and secular, including the arts.
4 Divine Energy, Creative, Dynamic Power that permeates all and is expressed in the feminine.
5 Hindu Goddess of Wealth.
6 'Maha' means 'great' and 'Ishwari' means 'Goddess', so Maheshwari is the Supreme Goddess in Hinduism.
7 Kali is a feminine form of the Sanskrit word 'kala', meaning 'time'. It also means 'black'. Kali is therefore always represented as black and is known as 'She who is the Mother of time'. Kali as Shakti is life energy. She is the destroyer of demons.
8 'Mother' in the Hindi language.

Cross-cultural barriers

Cross-cultural barriers – we tried to tear them down.
We looked at preconceptions,
at prejudice and fear,
and understood a little,
we've all got them lurking near.

Cross-cultural barriers – they needn't be abroad!
We thought about our neighbours,
our children and our friends.
They all have cultures not like ours.
They all have different trends.

Cross-cultural barriers – a case of them and us.
And if you're in, you're us, of course,
and what we do is right.
But if you're them, it's obvious,
you're odd, you're wrong, you're out!

Cross-cultural barriers seen from the other side,
a different perspective, for now it's us and them.
And they, of course, get all things right,
and peering through the barriers see,
that those who're wrong – it's we!

Cross-cultural barriers can mean safety, or a threat.
We need to tear them down.
To understand each other,
to love the stranger's ways
and fully live the truth that he is
    just
      another
         brother!

Geraldine Witcher, England

Beatitudes for interfaith families

(Matthew 5.3–12)

1. Blessed are the interfaith spouses, who, aware of the limits of their individual spiritual experience, are open to the God-experience of their partners who belong to another religion; they shall reign with God.

2. Blessed are the interfaith families who mourn because there is no room for them in the religious traditions and families of their birth; they shall be comforted.

3. Blessed are the interfaith couples who in humility risk the darkness of moving with the Spirit; they shall inherit the Earth.

4. Blessed are the interfaith couples who hunger and thirst for a communion that respects and is enriched by the unique spiritual gifts each partner brings; they shall be satisfied.

5. Blessed are the merciful interfaith couples whose pain of their aloneness moves them to work with religious authorities to expand their understanding of God and our relationship with God through our 'Kin-dom'; they shall know mercy.

6. Blessed are the interfaith parents who dare to teach their children to centre themselves on the 'I AM' who goes beyond all human boundaries and limitations; they shall see God.

7. Blessed are the peacemakers who offer support to interfaith couples and celebrate God's gift of love to them, as part of reconciling the whole world to God; they shall be called daughters and sons of God.

8. Blessed are interfaith spouses when they insult you and persecute you and utter all kinds of slander against you because you have married a person of another religion; on you God's favour rests. This is how the prophets who lived before you were persecuted.

Astrid Lobo Gajiwala, India

Interfaith worship for peace in the Middle East

People who are leading worship light candles.

1 Peter 3.8–12

Finally, all of you, have unity of spirit, sympathy, love for one another, a tender heart, and a humble mind. Do not repay evil for evil or abuse for abuse; but, on the contrary, repay with a blessing. It is for this that you were called – that you might inherit a blessing. For 'Those who desire life and desire to see good days, let them keep their tongues from evil and their lips from speaking deceit; let them turn away from evil and do good; let them seek peace and pursue it. For the eyes of the Lord are on the righteous, and his ears are open to their prayer. But the face of the Lord is against those who do evil.'

Let us pray

We pray for the innocent victims of violence in the Middle East; for the civilians who have lost their lives in recent hostilities; for the adults whose lives are dominated by the politics of fear; for the children whose innocence has been taken from them by bombs and bullets; for all who have come to live by violence and who find it an inevitability of life and death; for those who clamour for revenge while others call for forgiveness; for those who would exchange the nonsense of retribution for the healing and wholeness of authentic love that seeks to redeem the world from the core of its broken heart to the outer limits of the universal Spirit.

All: **May we learn how to have love**
        in our hearts
        and faith in one another
        so that in God
        we may seek to be his servants,
        to do his will
        and see his glory in the world. Amen.

People present are invited to light candles.

Andrew Clitheroe, England

We are one

We are all travelling on the same journey,
walking along parallel paths;
seeking after spiritual truth,
searching for One who'll make sense of our world,
longing for inner peace.

**Response: We are travellers on the same journey,
seeking, searching, longing.**

We are all travelling on the same journey,
walking along parallel paths;
seeking out ways to understand one another,
searching for ways we can work together,
longing for peace in the world.

**Response: We are travellers on the same journey,
seeking, searching, longing.**

We are all travelling on the same journey,
walking along parallel paths;
let us reach out to each other,
let us link hands together,
let us travel our journey as one.

Response: Reach out (Put hands out towards people next to us)
Link hands (Link hands with them)
We are one (Stand with hands still linked)
We are one (Still standing, hands still linked, raise arms
and shout joyfully)

*Note: The last response could be repeated as often as wished as we move
round and reach, link and shout with different people.*

Heather Johnston, Scotland

We come by many different paths

We come by many different paths,
Each certain that our way is true.
As sisters, brothers let us talk,
A way to peace is overdue.
Caged in a creed, we think we've caught
The source of all that is to be,
But God cannot be this confined:
The Spirit's flying, wild and free!

We think that we alone have found
The secret goal of all the earth;
We make our rules, oppress the weak,
With shackles hold them from their birth.
Within four walls we idolize
The treasures of our certainty.
We worship all that we have made.
Outside God sits in poverty.

So, prophets of this present age
Disturb us in our arrogance
To let the Spirit freely blow,
To offer love's extravagance.
For love can shake our self-conceit,
Tear up each creed, each guarantee;
Confronting cant and human pride,
God demonstrates love's quality.

Suggested tune: London (Kettering), 'He Leadeth Me'

Andrew Pratt, England

A prayer for blessing

Lord of my life,
bless me and in
blessing me,
bless others, too. Amen.

Andrew Clitheroe, England

124

Christ in the high street

In church we share the bread and wine as we have often done,
The people in the high street wonder what is going on.

And yet they too take wine and bread as ordinary food,
they are the sharers in a world which once was reckoned good.

Of course they are imperfect (as applies to me and you),
they search for symbols, just like us, as 'figures of the true'.

Christ in his hands took bread and wine, earthly and commonplace;
the act of giving thanks transformed them into means of grace.

For nothing in this world is as it really ought to be,
the good news is, God loves it still and works to set it free.

So when we meet in church around the table of the Lord,
partaking of the bread and wine according to his word,

think also of those other hours, the ordinary days,
we mingle with the crowd and share their ordinary ways.

Most of them have no place for church and rarely do they pray;
our feet and lips are Christ to them in what we do and say.

Our act of penitence and faith before the altar shown
is re-enacted day by day in workplace and at home.

There is a vast communion where the common is made new;
God is not only in the church but in the high street too.

John Adamson Brown, England

What has God done in your life?

You ask me to talk of God and all that he has done in my life,
and I look away, embarrassed,
unable to meet your eyes.

You talk of signs and wonders, miracles, calls;
I know only loneliness and despair.
You talk of assurance, adoption, love;
I know only desperation and blind hope.

You talk of God laughing with you in your joy;
I have only known him touching me in pain,
reaching out to sustain me yet another mile,
yet another hurdle, yet another day.

I have known precious moments of feeling God beside me,
of visions of his Son in glory,
yet mostly I feel that God is transcendent,
not immanent.

You ask me what he has done for me:
he has helped me to survive thus far
he has given me a reason to live
he has led me to my husband
he has called me here;
I do not know why.
At times I long to break free,
to forget the pain and drudgery of living.

Where is God the Father with his outstretched arms
awaiting the return of the Prodigal?
Where is the God of love in all this pain?

You ask me to talk of what God has done for me;
it is no pathway, blazing with glory, reflecting his love,
it is an endless slog,
through an endless tunnel.
What God has done for me is that I am still here.
Still fighting.

Still living.

A.K. Heathcoat, England

Build your world

God of our longing,
hear our prayers,
protect our dreams
and listen to our silent hopes.

Deal gently with our pain,
speak to our sadness
and remove the barriers
that imprison our spirit.

Shed your light
where shadows are cast,
that we may feel your warmth
and know your presence.

Give us courage
to hold fast to our vision
that we may build your world
and create our future.

*Annabel Shilson-Thomas/
CAFOD, England*

Awareness

As each leaf breathes,
as each flower exhales:
help us not to choke our
     neighbours.

As each bee hums,
as each bird sings:
help us not to deafen our
     neighbours.

As each dormouse squeaks,
as each bittern booms:
help us not to extinguish our
     neighbours.

As each raindrop falls,
as each tide rises:
help us not to drown our
     neighbours.

As each isotope decays,
as each cloud converges:
help us not to overwhelm our
     neighbours.

As we each consume,
as we each dispose:
help us to be aware of our
     neighbours.

Janet Lees, England

127

Lights in the darkness

Reflecting on the start of a new religious year for Christians, following the horrors of the calendar year for citizens around the globe, a father writes to his sons about those who have been lights in the darkness for him.

Dear Dominic and Gregory

We have just returned from the most beautiful candlelit service for Advent at Blackburn Cathedral. Its imagery has stirred in me a strong impulse to write to the two of you as you drift off to sleep. First, however, I must pick up your scattered clothes which lie on the floor in front of me.

I'm not sure what the cathedral congregation made of you, Dominic, dressed as Darth Vader, or you, Gregory, dressed as Luke Skywalker, or your friend, James, who wore a Captain Scarlet costume, but the fact that the three of you are attracted to such characters is, I think, very revealing.

Before the service, as the three of you enacted your 'pretend' battles between good and evil, they seemed an oddly appropriate preface to a procession that was all about light conquering darkness. Yet I couldn't help thinking that the world whose horizons grow bigger for the three of you each day is in fact so bleak and dark right now.

There was a stage when we could shelter you from this. Make sure that we watched the TV news when you were in bed. Hide the front page of the newspaper if the photographs were too grim. But these days you know all about what a tsunami can do to destroy human communities, what it means for young men with wives – and even young children – to blow people up on the Tube you've travelled on so many times, or the havoc that an earthquake can wreak for the world's poorest citizens in a place that everyone soon forgets.

You've seen pictures of the crying babies in Darfur, the bulldozed homes in Zimbabwe, the concrete wall chopping up the Holy Land. You've heard the screams of the grieving and helpless in Iraq, the angry in Paris and in Birmingham, and even, sometimes, as we've sped home on a weekend night from some event in Blackburn.

Your mother and I cannot hide you from reality any longer. At six and five you're too aware of the world for that. Though we would wish that it was otherwise, you go to a school which is dominated almost exclusively by white people. Very few of Blackburn's Muslims are educated alongside you. Most of them go to other schools that are sometimes as exclusively Muslim as your school is monochromely white. Which means that day by day all sorts of unhelpful stereotypes are doubtless being reinforced within each of you, at a subliminal and formative level. It also means that you are being made painfully aware of the degree to which racism eats away at the foundations of the society within which you are growing up.

Again, we cannot shield you from this. But we can try to temper, even counter, reality with hope. And it is this hope into which you were caught up this evening. I could see you from my canon's stall, transfixed by the beauty of worship at its best. Candlelight gradually sweeping through the cathedral as it will have done on Advent Sunday in churches throughout the world – words and music emphasizing the idea that human sin and suffering never have the last word which belongs to God, to love.

I could see your eyes, dazzled by the beauty and peacefulness of the whole occasion, as you drank in the warmth and quiet assurance it sought to convey to all who were there. And it made me all the more determined to share with you the many experiences your mother and I have had which bear testament to that old truth which somehow summed up the service's message: 'It is always better to light a candle than to curse the darkness.'

As you increase in years, how I want to tell you about the people who've done just that, struck a match, lit a candle for me and for others, most often against all the odds.

I remember, for instance, a remarkable friend of ours, Myra Osrin, whose time as the Director of the Cape Town Holocaust Centre soon comes to an end. I'll never forget that she was the first person to phone me after I'd written a newspaper article very critical of the antisemitism that has bedevilled the Church for 2,000 years. A disease that has caused Jews to endure so much terrible pain and suffering. A cancer that is present today when Jewish gravestones in Birmingham are daubed with swastikas. That phone-call to show solidarity was a godsend. A light amidst the darkness of all the hate mail that followed it and the vitriol of some of my fellow Christians that came soon after. It was the start of a friendship which I value so deeply with a person who has spearheaded the creation of one of Africa's most extraordinary and evocative museums, a museum built to counter all vitriol and bile.

It will be friendships with such people that I want to encourage you to have. Friendships which break the bonds of any segregation you experience as you move through school into adulthood. Friendships which keep alive the truth that people who believe in different things can actually work together rather than fight each other.

I'll want to tell you about another amazing woman from our time in Cape Town. Her name is Vivien Harber and she's one of our greatest friends. She's the woman, Gregory, who baptized you at St George's Cathedral, where she's been the only woman priest for many years, and perhaps the very first person in the Church who treated me for who I was rather than for where I'd studied or worked.

She's just about to leave South Africa and to go to New Zealand to be with her family. I'll try to explain, one day, the cost that's involved in leaving the

129

country that's been your home for your whole life, especially when you've invested so much in helping to transform its segregated landscape.

But I'll also be wanting to tell you what makes a person like Vivien so special – why she's not only a model for what a priest but, more importantly, for what any human being should be like. I'll want you to know that her qualities, her ability to listen to people , which is such a rare thing – the fact that she's incapable of passing by a person who needs help, and the dignity and respect she accords to people whatever their background or circumstances – these are the Christ-like qualities that all religions at their best aspire to embrace but which few people of any religion ever attain. They are the qualities your mother and I so hope that you will wish to make your own.

But I'll also want you to know that both Myra and Vivien, for all their grace, their gentleness and kindness, are feisty, steely women. Women who've had to make it in what is still a man's world – a world where feuds invariably end in the most unfeminine of ways, with flashing fists, because this is how men so often sort out the world's problems.

Which is why I will also be telling you about a more recent colleague and friend in Blackburn, Anjum Anwar, a remarkable Muslim woman, who has had to make it in a religious culture more dominated by men than most. She's the person with whom I walk as often as the two of us can manage to do so, to show our fellow citizens that if a white priest with a dog collar and a Muslim woman in a hijab are seen chatting together the world won't implode! I'll want you to know just how tenacious she is in seeking to help people overcome their prejudice and ignorance. The way in which through sheer persistence she makes people face the need to deal with difference through dialogue and conversation rather than monologue and conflict.

I'll hope that you can somehow acquire her ability to get people who would not otherwise talk to one another to do so. Because, as your mother and I have said several times recently, the world into which you are emerging is going to need that skill as much as any other.

But for now, as I fold away the remnants of Darth Vader and Luke Skywalker, I simply hope and trust that enough of the force we humans call love can be with you, so that one day you yourselves will draw inspiration, like us, from a Jew, a Christian and a Muslim, and help to create a world where difference is never seen to be a human problem but rather, a God-given asset to be celebrated and cherished.

All my love,
Daddy

Chris Chivers, England

Chapter Six

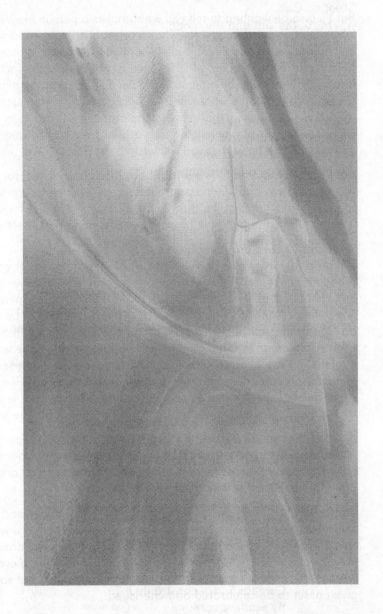

Set us all free

Belonging to each other

Creating God,
you make the sun and the moon,
you make the day and the night,
you make the land and the sea,
you make the plants and the animals.

Creating God,
you make boys and girls,
you make us young and old,
you make us black and white,
you make us gay and straight.

Creating God,
you make us fathers and mothers,
you make us brothers and sisters,
you make us sons and daughters,
you make us aunts and uncles.

Thank you that you have created us to belong to the earth.
Thank you that you have created us to belong to each other.
Thank you that you have created us to belong to you. Amen.

Clare McBeath, England

Asylum seekers

They live under the shadow of
A two-edged sword: in a place of safety
And a state of fear. The rules
Ensure *we* are kept safe; *our* fear
Defines our hospitality,
Keeps them on edge.
Compassion is constrained
By prudent care.

Could we, instead of seeing problems,
Begin to recognize the gifts they bring,
And be enriched by their humanity?

Ann Lewin, England

Bring light into dark places

Lord of love,
we thank you for the fact that we are here –
gathered from our various places
in our diverse city.

Lord of light,
we ask that you will guide our thoughts,
guide our future actions
so that,
with your love,
we shall bring light into the dark places
of the lives of women . . .
men . . .
children . . .
who need active care and compassion
to enable them to live . . .
to live . . .
to grow in a strange land . . .
reach their potential
and know that there is love
in this dark world.

Geoffrey Duncan, England

Rainbow people

Creator God, you have made us your rainbow people,
called to share your God colours in the world.
Make us greedy to receive your bread and wine
in order to hold fantastic parties
to which all are invited and made welcome.
To us now, O God,
bring your hope,
bring your love,
bring your light.

Lythan Nevard, England

133

The fugitive

You scrambled from the train
at dead of night –
from its dark underbelly
finally at rest;
you gasped and stretched,
relieved yourself towards an alien tree,
and then stood, wondering . . .
what would this place hold for you –
a welcome?

No, only subterfuge and fear,
for here is no place for you,
a man without papers.

For papers are all
in civilized places –
different faces close to those
without them –
papers are the stamp of truth,
the proof of expectation.
But you are not expected here
and will be hounded out,
just as your mother country
hounded you –

What will you do?
Where will you go
in this dark place
whose people and whose tongue
you do not know?
They will not credit you
with gifts to give –
they will not give you
any place to live . . .
They will hound you,
hound you –

like a fugitive.

Margot Arthurton, England

Refugees

They stream across our screens
Balancing impossible burdens;
The remnants of their lives
Tied up in bundles.
Yet what we see is nothing
To the burden they carry
In their hearts:
Loss, pain and fear.

Ann Lewin, England

Here stands a stranger, who is she?

Here stands a stranger, who is she?
We do not know. Whom do we see,
someone who threatens you and me?
Is she a foe, or friend?

Here stands a person, young or old,
seeking asylum, so we're told.
How does he fit your frame or mould?
Is he your foe or friend?

Here stands a child: assess her need.
What should we offer so we heed
her cry of hunger, so we feed
this child? This foe? This friend?

Here stands a person, this time, you.
The choice is yours. What will you do
to ask this stranger in, or sue
this foe, who could be friend?

Here is a mirror, see your face.
What do you offer: hatred, grace,
now in this very time and place,
to Christ you call your friend?

Andrew Pratt, England

God whom we fail to see

A woman from Pakistan seeking leave to remain in England said, 'Don't send me back to my country; they will torture me again.'

'If I have money, what does it do me if I have lost my husband?
If I have money, what does it do me if I have lost my family?
If I have money, what does it do me if I have lost my country?'

God, whom we fail to see in the faces and lives of those different from us,
stir us to see you in stranger, alien and foreigner in our midst.
Stir us to act with you in welcoming and protecting the outcast in our road.
Stir us to speak with you in resisting the merciless acts of rejection against the Other in our society.
Stir us to live as if people matter to us as much as our church building, our traditions and our treasures.
Stir us up until you delight in our hospitality in Britain towards others and you. Amen.

Kate Gray, England

Witch and widow

The Witch of Endor (Old Testament) and The Widow of Nain (New Testament) are both connected by being from the same geographical area yet they have very different lives. They are brought together by their connection with the earth.

Wonder witch and weary widow,
you never even met.
Woven together by place not in person,
in time and in stone you're not set.
Let's look at the stories,
find what is hidden.
Uncover, unearth greatest depths.
Let's listen to their silence
and find buried treasure
by mystery, magic and madness.

Kate Gray, England

No

No.
No blacks no pakis.
No.
No girls (on our team).
No women (in our ancient and privileged club).
No.
No poofs no queers.
A dismal November of living.

But with the solstice, the sun's standing,
comes celebration of a new beginning,
the Light
of a world gone stale and dark.

Around Jesus there turns and shifts
a brightness, a colour pattern
of human humanity,
variegated, diverse.

Not no, but yes –
yes to the foreigner,
yes to the woman,
yes to the outcast, the pariah, the leper.

The only no was to hypocrisy,
to exclusivity of financial or religious status.

After this no to no,
after this yes,
this warmth and light,
sun stops standing, and moves on
into Spring, New Life.
Yes.

Janet Wootton – with homage to Thomas Hood, England

Portrayal

I never thought of grief as barbed wire
until I saw it painted around your heart:

muscular pulses punctuated with tears,
fencing in tomorrow. A sharp reminder

of fear that still hangs on battlefields,
the slow unravelling hurt borne by families,

the scarring of Our Lord. Your resurrected loss
portrayed as both obstacle and shield.

Eve Jackson, England

Cross-dressing God

Cross-dressing God,
known to us in the holiness of our longings
and the ecstasies of our bodies,
unmask us and we will unmask your Church,
meeting each other face to face
to set all people free.

Cross-dressing God,
who goes with us as we parade with pride
and uncloset ourselves as your people,
unburden us and we will unburden your Church,
freeing each other step by step
to set all people free.

Cross-dressing God,
known to us in the destabilizing of our sexualities
and countering the heteropatriarchies,
undo the damage done to us and we will undo it in your Church,
queering and healing each other one by one
to set all people free.

Kate Gray, England

A country we could share

For two voices

Voice one: Is this our country and a holy land more than others?

Voice two: The woman who lives next door never speaks to me and her face is always covered.

Voice one: Is this our country and a land grander with history?

Voice two: The boy with a turban in the church school visits my shop every day.

Voice one: Is this our country where all should learn the language?

Voice two: The man from the takeaway speaks with strange words I don't understand.

Voice one: Is this our country to defend against the terrors within?

Voice two: The call to prayer sounds beautiful now we don't hear the church bell.

Voice one: Is this our country where churches crumble and are bought for carpet showrooms?

Voice two: The buildings trace our hopes and fears with walls to keep us in.

Voice one: Is this our country any more – where neighbours, schools and shops have changed?

Voice two: Is this a country we could share – where sights and sounds show us new ways?

Both voices: Is this a country we could share?

Both voices: If not here then where?

Kate Gray, England

The chain

Imprisoned.
Heavy chains
interlocking and entwined,
clinging, biting, marking their
    impress.
No beginning and no ending.
No escape.

And yet,
only one link needs to be broken
to set me free.
Which one, Lord?

Ros Murphy, England

Freedom and unity

From the ancestors we bring
new worlds in old,
searching
reaching
toward love
toward life
for identity
for **freedom**.

In the common spirit
we live.

So the drum beats on
in our hearts, in our minds.
We are one.

And the drum beats on.
Fill our hearts, fill our minds
as we search
as we reach
in our freedom from the past
in our freedom in the now
in our free
        dom
in the king
        dom
in the One.

Claire Smith, Guyana/USA

Divisions and unity

(A response to racism)

The Berlin Wall has fallen,
the Iron Curtain has disintegrated,
yet still the world is divided.
We divide ourselves by age,
by sex,
by race,
by dialect,
by geography,
by attitude,
until we are alone.

Alone, in a select group,
a group of those who reflect
    our own views,
who confirm our perceptions,
who shore up our own prejudices,
and there we stagnate,
not growing,
not learning,
simply reflecting each other's views,
being mirrors for our
    friends' opinions.

When someone disagrees
they are rejected,
ostracized,
for they have dared to make waves,
they have dared to shatter
    the mirror.

Even Christians divide;
we split into denominations,
suspicious of each other,
outwardly united,
inwardly segregated.
We ignore the Christ who unites,
who crosses all barriers
and breaks them down,
who calls everyone friend.

His love extends to us all,
every stranger we see,
whatever their colour,
their age,
their sex,
their opinions,
in him they are our neighbour,
yet we treat them as enemies
because they have the potential to
    disrupt our lives.

Don't divide – unite in Christ.

A.K. Heathcoat, England

141

There, there, you'll soon get over it

There, there, you'll soon get over it;
chin up, flint face; turn the other cheek,
there's always tomorrow,
smooth words, empty epithets, groundless hope
doled out, lashings of it.

There, there, you'll soon get over it,
and so will we when you do.
So, do me a favour, get a life,
go out more often, stretch your legs, take the air,
taste the salt in it.

There, there, you'll soon get over it,
Time's a great healer, look on the bright side,
smooth words, empty epithets, groundless hope.
Tight bound in clinking chains, there is no up,
no yesterday, no today, no tomorrow, no getting,
no stretching, no time,
pinned down, close confined.

There, there, you'll soon get over it.
Like Jesus got over getting sold, being betrayed,
mocked and done to death.
There, there, you'll soon get over it,
and if you can't, run before I catch you
and bring you back to where you started
the wretched, draining, tearing,
frightening journey . . .

David Isherwood, England

Security – thanksgiving and confession

God of the generations who've gone before us,
we give you thanks for our sense of identity,
forged from the mix of family and culture,
from nationality and religion.
**We confess that we have sometimes
denied the identity of others
and have sought to make others in our own image.**

God of our turbulent, insecure world,
we give you thanks when life feels safe and secure,
for the ways we can plan for difficult times
and plan for our future.
**We confess that we have sometimes
hidden behind our policies and pensions
and buffered ourselves from the pain of the world.**

God who is birthing new life,
we give you thanks for the differences
and dissonance that give life its vibrancy and colour,
its energy and excitement.
**We confess that we have sometimes
preferred the drabness of the familiar
and denied others their dreams and aspirations.**

Clare McBeath, England

143

Overcoming obstacles

A place of grandeur, ceremony, chandeliers and suits! An address, 'all very p.c. of course', of humbling gratitude, talk of selfless acts, overcoming obstacles and heroism. The finest food and wine.

The ordinary speaking of their surprise at this recognition. Every one a story to tell. Not their own tale, but a tale of meeting the needs of others.

A man speaks. He describes his own journey, fleeing his home and country to build a new life. A man whose homeland is Somalia. Blinded and disabled by a landmine, arriving in this country, a place he cannot see, where people spoke a language he could not understand. The obstacles he has overcome. Ten years on, he reads his story in English from a sheet of Braille. Behind him a man is interpreting the words with his hands to a small group.

I'm next to a lady I saw arriving earlier when the doors opened of the cold steel box. She looked down for a moment at those ascending the grand marble staircase with its fine pictures and statues. As she arrived at the door she took her sticks, arose from her chair and entered the room so proudly.

A man with a stick, a man with a limp, an elderly woman 'all doing so well' . . .

The moment of recognition, praise and applause, the photographers' flash . . .

But this moment was flawed, for there was one final hurdle in all of these journeys before that final moment of recognition.

The mayor in his glory, standing on his platform, inviting these few to celebrate the moment . . . Up those steps!

Michael Watson, England

Making a difference

God of an ever-evolving universe,
a butterfly wing beats on the other side of the earth,
a cartoon published in a small country in Europe causes riots,
power stations spew out emissions of greenhouse gases,
a hotter planet causes drought and famine,
melting ice caps cause floods and disease,
Exaggerated intelligence sparks deadlock and conflict.
**All around us we can see that small events
can change the course of history.**

God of our ever-evolving lives,
a new family moving into a street, learning the language,
house prices rising and regeneration plans delayed,
a factory closing causing unemployment and loss of esteem,
a school valuing creativity and encouraging potential,
a change in job to allow time for family,
the conception of a new life changing priorities.
**All around us we can see that small decisions
can change the course of our lives.**

God who calls us to decision making,
help us to see how a simple smile can brighten a day,
how befriending a newcomer builds community,
that eating a balanced diet helps keep us healthy,
and taking an interest gives the next generation a role model.
Help us to see a job well done brings satisfaction,
that making time for family and friends enriches our lives.
**We thank you for the choices we have,
that in our own small way we can make a difference.**

Clare McBeath, England

Sale price!

(Dolly and Daisy, or Dave and Don – or any combination of these two, plus a Narrator)

Narrator Sale price! Buy cheap! Bargain basement! Double discount! Special offer!

Pause

Dolly There used to be hundreds of mill chimneys round here.

Daisy I remember! It was like a forest when you looked down from here.

Dolly And the noise when all the clogs went clattering down the cobbles – if you weren't awake by then, that soon woke you up.

Daisy That – and the factory hooter!

Dolly Mind, you had to be there on time, or they locked you out of the gates.

Daisy And those mill owners were slave drivers.

Dolly Long hours.

Daisy Low pay.

Dolly Mucky working conditions.

Daisy Smoky chimneys.

Dolly Everywhere black . . .

Daisy . . . even the buildings.

Dolly Aye! We're better off now the mills have gone.

Daisy Nice clean buildings.

Dolly No more mill owners with fancy cars and country mansions.

Daisy No clogs and factory hooters.

Dolly It's just a shame that our kids can't get work round here any more.

Daisy And there's far too many folk living on 'the Social'.

Dolly But the clothes they bring from the Far East are really cheap.

Daisy Well, that'll be because they don't have to pay their workers very much.

Dolly D'you think they have mill chimneys over there now?

Pause

Narrator Sale price! Buy cheap! Bargain basement! Double discount! Special offer!

Marjorie Dobson, England

Blood

A dark stain blemishes the
   blankets of snow
covering Mount Ruapehu.
An ugly scar on perfect whiteness
tears of Mount Ruapehu.
In shadow, black, blood red
in sunlight.
Fresh blood oozing from wounds.
Innocent blood spilled, not in war
nor accident,
cut lips, broken noses, bleeding ears.
Broken bodies of abused women
   and children
of Ruapehu.

Mighty mountain, guardian of
   the people.
Sleeping under drifting snow
until
blood seeps through
   ancient crevasses.
The mountain shakes in rage
whipping snow into storms.
Wild winds howl round the summit.
A great fire ignites in the deep.

The mountain sighs,
restless, scaring the people.
There will be no peace
until these people,
the people of Ruapehu,
wash away the bloody stain
with their tears falling like rain.

      Wendy Ward,
Aotearoa New Zealand

Human beings, bought or bartered

Human beings, bought or bartered,
kept apart by race or creed,
chained by culture or religion,
when, O God, can we be freed?

God, we need your rich compassion,
Spirit, fire your love on earth,
bringing mercy to our judgements,
recognizing human worth.

Help us, God, to love each
   neighbour,
building through each law and act
justice in our legislation,
changing mercy into fact.

Take away the bonds that bind us
then, in hope of liberty,
we will work and strive for freedom
and for human dignity.

      Andrew Pratt, England

147

Imagine . . .

On the evening of 7 July 2005 I was at the Town Hall for a meeting of our Muslim Christian Forum. As the news of the London bombings began to sink in we stood in silence side by side – words came later.

Imagine,
imagine there are no countries
imagine there are no races
imagine there are no cultures
imagine there are no religions
nothing to kill for
nothing to die for
no World War II
no London bombs.

Imagine everyone in identical dress
imagine everyone eating from one menu
imagine everyone living in monochrome cities
imagine everyone believing one creed
nothing to celebrate
nothing to mourn
nothing to spark debate
nothing to dream.

For there is no heaven while wars rage
there is no heaven while bombs shatter lives
there is no heaven while global warming goes unchecked
there is no heaven while some hoard and others go hungry
but there is also no heaven when everything is uniform
there is no heaven when life all tastes the same
there is no heaven when there is only one human habitat
there is no heaven when we are not free to hold our own beliefs.

Imagine,
imagine there are catwalks full of exotic clothes
imagine there are menus of gastronomic delight
imagine there are landscapes diverse as fantasy worlds
imagine there are religions to make every day a festival celebration
everything to preserve life for
everything to live for
where we become friends with those who are different
where we enrich life by sharing food and customs across the divides.

For this is the taste of God's world we want to celebrate
this is the canvas painted by God that is bursting with colour
this is the love of knowledge of God who cannot be confined to one scripture
this is the wisdom of God who invites us to share in Shanti
in Salaam
in Shalom
in Pacem
in Peace.

Clare McBeath, England

God of love, we welcome you

Renewing God, give us the strength and courage to live this day in the power of your Spirit. May we live as a community of your people whose lives witness to others of your love. Let our deeds match our prayers and bring us out of our comfort zones so we know what it is to live the gospel with our whole lives.
Response: God of love, we welcome you.

Reigning king, help us to know more fully that your kingship was about true humility. We want to be people who are humble yet know the power of the Spirit in your resurrection. Help us to share in the resurrection by making your love known to those who feel unloved or unlovable. Enable us to be humble yet bold people of the gospel when we share your love.
Response: God of love, we welcome you.

Creative Spirit, we recognize you in the ability to paint, sing, draw, sculpt, write, act and dance. There are many artists of life in our society and in different cultures. We pray for their strengthening and inspiration that they may continue to glorify you and help us to worship you by using their talents. We praise you for them, artist and author of the universe.
Response: God of love, we welcome you.

Laughing God, we thank you for giggling and great guffaws, for laughter among friends and for humour in life. We ask that you will make us more sensitive to those whose lives lack laughter and joy. Be with those who are too serious and use us to nudge them to smile a little more and see the release which comes from joy.
Response: God of love, we welcome you.

Kate Gray, England

Intercession

God, who holds all suffering
and all joy in your being,
whose spirit gives life to all creation,
why do we pray our prayers for others?
Every hair of every head,
every feather, every blade of grass,
all life is known and dear to you.
You do not need us to tell you to care.

It is our own hearts and minds we open
when we pray beyond ourselves.
We pray out the commandment to love.
How can we pray without caring enough to learn
what life means for those in our prayers?
How can we not love those we pray for?
How can we love you, God whom we have not seen
except in your creation?

Diana Roberts, Aotearoa New Zealand

Prayer for the oldest trade in the world

When children are sleeping in the next room,
when there are school fees to pay
when pimps pressurize and push people around,
God help us
work to set all people free.

When dirty needles share numbness and disease,
when neighbours know and choose not to care,
when a client uses fists and fear,
God help us
work to set all people free.

When economies depend on people's exploitation,
when Bible bashers quote and condemn,
when death-sex power seems almost dominant,
God help us
work to set all people free.

Kate Gray, England

What a way to earn a living

On the coast of Ghana sit two 'castles', prisons for many millions of Africans who were captured into slavery in past centuries – 15 million transported to the Americas. It was on this trade in humans as commodities that wealth in Europe was built. Over the cells where the slaves were imprisoned waiting for deportation, was a chapel. Christians worshipped God while directly below, right under their feet, those being sold into slavery languished in chains and in horror of those dungeons.

From the brilliant African light,
deep into these dark filthy cells,
we crowd together retching from the stench of naked flesh against flesh,
tightly packed, containers of trade for overseas.
One on top of another, gasping for the free air of our homeland.
We stare at the grill above
as shards of blistering light
shear our black faces.
We see the dancing feet
and hear the stranger's strange songs.

> Out from the burning intensity of African heat
> to our cool chapel to sing praises to God.
> This dark and filthy land
> with its fearsome black dogs
> causes us to sing the psalms of release and freedom.
> The animals underneath our feet,
> rescued from their alien land
> will give us a little wealth and reward.
> We look down at those white startled eyes
> repelled by their hoary breath.

Who might these strangers be,
who have brought us here?
What will they do to us –
offer us up for sacrifice to their gods?

> Who might these animals be,
> who have brought us here?
> What will they do to us
> – if they ever escape –
> offer us up to their primitive gods?

God – save us from this place.
Lord, out of the depths I have called to you.

*Martin Hazell, England, adapted from a message to the Churches,
World Alliance of Reformed Churches Council in Accra 2004*

'My chains fell off, my heart was free'

(Honouring Minarapa Rangihatuake,
a Methodist Maori who took the gospel to his
people at Wellington, New Zealand in June 1839)

Your life in Taranaki was devastated
when as a young man you were taken prisoner
by a raiding party of Ngapuhi from the distant north.
You became one of their slaves.

Methodists from England established
a mission station amongst Ngapuhi
and urged them to set their slaves free.
You were liberated and went to
the Methodist mission station at Mangungu.
There the missionary John Bumby took you under his wing
and equipped you to be a missionary to your own people.

A journey south in 1839 with Bumby
and fellow missionary John Hobbs
took you to the Great Harbour of Tara (Wellington)
where some of your Taranaki kin had migrated.
You prepared the way for Bumby and Hobbs to come ashore,
meet your people, and introduce them to the gospel.

When Bumby and Hobbs went away,
you stayed to minister to your people,
proclaiming a gospel message of peace.
You built the first church (a raupo hut)
at Te Aro Pa, provided regular worship,
and preached the gospel.
You stayed till your elders called you home
to Taranaki to minister to your own.

In 1840 the first settlers from Britain arrived.
In time they dispossessed the people
of Te Aro of their land,
their gardens and burial grounds.
You stood as an advocate for your people,
but the odds were stacked against you.
Within a few years Te Aro Pa was gone,
and your people once again dispersed.

A hundred years later the Methodists,
no longer Maori but people of British stock,
erected a stone memorial to that first service
of worship on the site that had once been Te Aro Pa.
Bumby's and Hobbs' names were carved into the stone.
But your name was not there.

It was to be another 50 years
before that wrong was put right.
Your faith descendants,
a small congregation of Maori Methodists,
insisted your name be carved into that stone,
to honour your life and work.

Did you sing with Charles Wesley,
'My chains fell off,
My heart was free,
I rose, went forth,
and followed thee'?

John Roberts, Aotearoa New Zealand

We cannot be dismissive

We cannot be dismissive
amid the dark despair
that leaves a nation broken
for Christ is crippled there.

God give us fresh compassion
and courage in this plight,
to live the words of justice
we cry into the night.

We need to offer healing,
to build a sense of trust
where human lives are fractured
and hope is ground to dust.

God give us motivation,
we'll not succumb to fate,
we'll make our reparation,
the time is not too late.

Andrew Pratt, England

A litany of repentance and supplication

Lord God almighty, creator of all things, judge of all people, we confess with
sorrow and shame our ill-treatment of one another.
We do not love our neighbours as ourselves but instead use people for our
own ends, and our attitudes can cause terrible problems.
We ask for the gift of your Holy Spirit to make us aware of what we are
doing and to help us to change our ways.
Hear our cry, Lord,
and in your great mercy help us and set us all free.

Lord, when we are tempted to tell lies and to deceive people with false
promises in order to get them to do what we want,
hear our cry, Lord,
and in your great mercy help us and set us all free.

Lord, when we are tempted to use force, tempted to use mental and physical
violence and abuse in order to get people to do what we want,
hear our cry, Lord,
and in your great mercy help us and set us all free.

Lord, when we are tempted to oppress people to increase our own feelings
of self-importance, to exploit them to our own advantage,
hear our cry, Lord,
and in your great mercy help us and set us all free.

Lord, where our behaviour and ill-treatment of others have caused deep
bitterness and resentment,
hear our cry, Lord,
and in your great mercy help us and set us all free.

Lord, where people have been caused to fear and to hate,
hear our cry, Lord,
and in your great mercy help us and set us all free.

Lord, where we are enslaved by destructive cravings and habits,
hear our cry, Lord,
and in your great mercy help us and set us all free.

Lord Jesus, we ask for courage to stand in your name against the evil we
encounter both within ourselves and in the world.
Grant us, gracious Lord, a share in your compassion,
your generosity, your justice, your mercy, so that wrongs are righted,
wounds are healed, justice is done, and your truth does indeed set us all free,
for your love's sake.

Amen.

Pauline Bower, England

set all free

Gracious and liberating God

We pray to a God who with amazing grace has taken the initiative in reconciling us to himself. God reveals himself as one who leads his people from slavery in Egypt, and in Jesus proclaims release to captives and lets the oppressed go free.

Lift us beyond the burdens of pain and guilt

We ask that we are taken into new ways of being, not only that the burdens that constrain us be lifted. Pain is felt by those whose ancestors were enslaved and those who enslaved them; and pain continues in terms of impoverishment and disadvantage. Guilt is one of several shared emotions, related to shame, blame, anger, bitterness and desolation, which we pray we may transcend by God's healing power.

Build our memories into life-giving resolutions

Some memories are painful, recalling the hurts and discord of the past; other memories are happy and encouraging, and we are inspired by the witness and example of others. All memories, personal and corporate, are the blocks we can use to build together those things that are life-giving, and enable one another to be human beings fully alive . . . the glory of God.

Give us the vision of a new creation

If anyone is in Christ, there is a new creation, one in which we are reconciled to God and to one another. We are ministers of this reconciliation in a fragmented and disunited world.

Strengthen us to act for justice and human dignity

The spiritual experience of release from the slavery of sin takes us on to work for a better world, in which justice flows like a river, and every man, woman and child may flourish as those made in the image of God. Hence the imperative to act to end slavery now, in this generation.

And set all free.

Our hope is that we and the whole creation will be brought into the glorious liberty of the children of God.

'set all free', England

Living, loving Father of us all

Living, loving Father of us all,
Lord of time and space
we come before your throne of grace
with all those who in past times have
suffered the brutality, fear and injustice
of slavery, grieving with all those who
remember their anguish with pain and bitterness.
Merciful Lord,
grant us all your healing and your help.

Loving Lord God, holy and righteous,
we come before your throne of grace
with all those who have profited unjustly
from the slave trade and from the work
done by slaves; with all those who
received compensation for setting their
slaves free, and with the slaves who were left
to fend for themselves.
Merciful Lord,
grant us all your healing and your help.

Living Lord God, the Way, the Truth and the Life,
we come before your throne of grace
with all those who are enslaving people today
through false promises, trickery, force,
through having inherited them;
with all those who have been enslaved through
poverty, violence, inheritance, or
through having been captured.
Merciful Lord,
grant us all your healing and your help.

Living, loving Lord God, just and merciful,
we come before your throne of grace
with all the women who have been
sold, tricked and bullied into prostitution,
who are exploited as domestic servants;
with the children who are also forced
into the sex trade and into domestic service,
who struggle with heavy loads in mines,
who cart heavy stones to make roads,

who make bricks, carpets, clothes and other goods,
who are chained so that they cannot run away.
Merciful Lord,
grant us all your healing and your help.

Lord, the catalogue of misery and pain
is grim, and we are complicit in this either
because we are unaware of what is happening
or because we shut our minds to it.
Grant us grace to pay proper attention
to the conditions of life of other people;
to work to ensure that they are able to
live life to the full and receive just
recompense and reward for their work.
Merciful Lord,
**grant us all the understanding and the will
to change things for the benefit of all who
are enslaved.**

In Jesus' name. Amen.

Pauline Bower, England

Observer

I was an observer.
I was not on the front-line.
I was on my sofa
and you were on the box
in the corner of the room.
I saw your tears.
I heard you crying.
I saw you hug your children
as I cuddled mine.
I heard the politician's plans and promises.
I saw the aid workers, the queues,
the reporters, the bodies in mass graves.
I was an observer from my sofa.

God of hope, stir me up!
Make me as hungry for justice as you are.

Janet Lees, England

God of surprises

God of surprises, we see that Ruth dared
to stand for the people who needed her care;
though not with her 'own kind', she still chose to stay,
so shows us commitment: shall we walk her way?   Ruth 1–4

God of true Wisdom who wanders the streets
inviting us 'Come' to share wine and to eat
as Wisdom delights in the fruits of her stall,
so teach us your insight: full life is for all!   Proverbs 9.1–6

God of all people, the prophets proclaimed
your strength is your love, which can never be tamed;
and just as a mother would comfort each child
so you, God, embrace both the weak and the wild.   Isaiah 66.13

God of compassion, through Jesus you cried
for cities oppressed and for peace still denied;
you long to protect us, to be mother hen,
to heal all our hurting again and again.   Matthew 23.37

God of great feeling, whatever the cost
you search like a woman whose treasure is lost,
so teaching us all of your passionate will
to bring us together, that love be fulfilled.   Luke 15.8–9

Suggested tune: Slane

Graham Adams, England

Celebrate the Haystack Bicentennial

(Australian Tamil Christian Communities)

'That is my school!' exclaims a Tamil woman at a recent Haystack Celebration planning committee meeting in Melbourne, Australia. Her school, the Uduvil School pictured in the photo we are viewing, was the first school for women in Asia, she claims. Started by American Board missionaries, it provided education to her and other young women in India at a time when females were considered little more than family wealth in the form of dowries. Her education there changed her life. She proudly explains that the Uduvil School continues to provide education to women of Sri Lanka today.

In anticipation of the Haystack bicentenary, the Tamil Christian communities of Melbourne planned a celebration which was held at the Churches of Christ Theological College on 30 September 2006. This venue had been chosen because it was discovered that Global Ministries missionaries, Ana and Tod Gobledale, are currently serving there as chaplains. Prayers were shared at the respective Haystack Celebration events, and exchanged with the Williamstown UCC, USA. One of the prayers was written by the Revd S. Manopavan, a minister in the Uniting Church of Australia, originally from the American Ceylon Mission, Church of South India. It expresses the gratitude of so many people who have come through the American Board (now Global Ministries) institutions, schools and churches, and live in Australia today.

God of grace and God of love, it is with grateful hearts that we come before you as we reflect on our rich Christian heritage as Tamil Christians.
Two centuries ago, five college students were gripped by a deep sense of call to move out of their comfort zone in order to take their own experience of your love as revealed in your Son to be shared with those living in faraway countries around the unknown world of that time.
We thank you, O Lord, that you spoke to them so clearly in that storm that they accepted the trust you had placed on them.
Heavenly Father, we, the beneficiaries of their obedience, thank you for them and all who followed them in the mission field.
Accept our praise and thanks, O Lord, that today we are a people of your blessing, of enlightenment, of confidence, and above all a people of deep faith in your goodness. May our gratitude be commensurate with our desire to be obedient to your call to serve you and your people. Amen.

Ana & Tod Gobledale, Australia

Touch the truth

(A poem of land, roots and
identity)

It's hard to express
but the tumble of notions
creates a strange sense
of belonging and pride.
The story is shared
though the language is different;
the needs that unite
banish fears that divide.

Here in our searching
for roots and contentment,
parochial feelings
of culture and land,
we can but reflect
on all that is common:
a treasure to share
in the gift of each hand.

We are who we are
and our own past is sacred,
but never a source
of resentment and hate;
the silence of martyrs
is worth more than bullets:
the blood from the veins
gives a cross of great weight.

New curtains are torn
and new chances before us;
old Babels must fall
and the body made whole:
the bread of the broken
and wine for our healing,
a meal of forgiveness
of love once for all.

For we touch the truth,
when we hear the words
and accept the future lies
    in our hands;
and we speak of peace
and we thirst for love
and hunger that we
    all understand.

Stephen Brown, Scotland

Chapter Seven

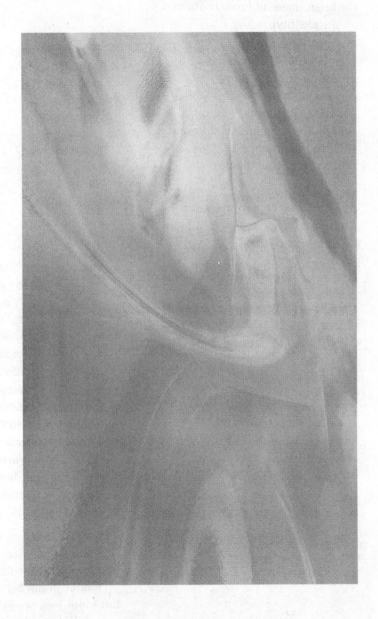

Peace – the urgent need for humankind

Atonement

my bread smells of
   distant gunsmoke;
my wine tastes of
   innocent blood.

in crunching down the crust
I feel
houses crushed;
   bridges bombed;
   roads and runways
   ground to bits.

in pouring out the wine
I hear
   children screaming – both
   Sarah and Hagar weeping;
   a million bare feet fleeing.

in the mix of
smoked bread and bloodied wine
I taste
   a gathering bitterness of
   ten teeth for a tooth;
   ten heads for an eye –
   an eternal tornado of
   rage and revenge.

unable – or unwilling –
   to out-shout the guns
   or cry out with both
   Sarah and Hagar
I filter from both bread and wine
   the smell of smoke
   the taste of blood;
I sweeten the bitter mix with
   What-can-I-do and
   This-is-the-sacrifice-
   I-must-make-to-the-god-
   of-TheWarOnTerror.

until – in no time –
I no longer smell
   the smoke;
I no longer taste
   the blood;
I no longer hear
   Hagar or Sarah;
but I feel
the earth tremble
beneath a million
   marching
      feet.

Norm S.D. Esdon, Canada

Father, forgive

When we are selfish, demand our own way,
angry, bring trouble with things that we say;
when we avoid those we don't understand,
thoughtless and won't lend a hand;
then we must turn and remember the words of Jesus:
'Father, forgive.'

Violence and hatred and war's evil hand,
families are fleeing, a grim, wasted land;
women are weeping and childhood is gone,
homeless, they just struggle on;
all we can do is remember the words of Jesus:
'Father, forgive.'

When life is hard as we try to do good,
overlooked, lied about, misunderstood;
if cries for justice are simply ignored,
there's someone who's been there before;
so we can turn and remember the words of Jesus:
'Father, forgive.'

Rose Reeve, England

Love one another

You gave birth to creation from your perfect love
From the deep rolling oceans, to mountains above.
Then you said to your people, 'One thing you must do:
Will you love one another as I have loved you?'

> *Chorus:*
> *Try to love one another as I have loved you;*
> *They're my long ago words that are simple but true.*
> *Will you follow these words of mine all your lives through?*
> *Will you love one another as I have loved you?*

Then you sent your own Son to show your perfect love;
Whatever they did to him, he would forgive.
He told all his disciples, 'There's one thing to do:
Will you love one another as I have loved you?'

> *Chorus*

As we travel this world showing anger and greed
So the time has now come for us all to take heed
Of your words that were spoken both simple and true:
'Will you love one another as I have loved you?'

> *Chorus*

Suggested tune: Dark Island

Heather Johnston, Scotland

Nageena

I want to sit and hold her,
rock and comfort her,
soothe her pain.

Not tell her 'It'll be all right.'

It won't ever be all right again,
not for her: damaged
beyond surgeon's repair
by ripping rapes; damaged
beyond therapist's aid
by hate-filled gang; damaged
beyond words – left mute,
a battered rag-doll, discarded.

I want to hold and comfort her
in silent love.

Abigail Joy Tobler, England

We should not live through this without a protest

We should not live through this without a protest,
the massacre of those who cannot fight.
O God, what is the purpose of this killing,
the warp of words when wrong is labelled right?

The women run, their children now are orphaned.
No land, no creed can justify this fact,
no god is author of this intervention,
our human anger drives the way we act.

O God, when you confronted human hatred,
you died abandoned by the ones you led,
yet reached to them with steadfast loving kindness;
you gave forgiveness while you hung and bled.

So help us face this present time, this moment,
where love and fear, where grace and judgement dwell,
give us the courage that we might be Christ-like,
to work for peace within this man-made hell.

Suggested tune: Intercessor

Andrew Pratt, England

Will we turn the other cheek?

And would we turn the other cheek?
While the bulldozers destroy our houses,
when our children play with toy guns and are shot by real bullets,
as our land is carved up by new highways but not for us to travel on,
and we feel the humiliation of the checkpoints every day.

And would we turn the other cheek?
If our land were under siege from neighbours denying our right just to be there,
when we all know family and friends killed or injured in suicide bombings,
and the young soldier captured in Gaza could be our son.

Holy Land! How, Holy Land?
While so divided by race, culture, belief and now by a Wall.
Break through, O God – Yahweh – Allah!
You teach us to turn the other cheek
not just in words, but in Jesus' whole life.
So, will we turn the other cheek?

Brian Ball, England

A prayer for an end to violence

God of life,
every act of violence in our world,
in our communities, between myself and others,
destroys a part of your creation.

Stir in my heart
a renewed sense of reverence
for all life.

Give me the vision to recognize your spirit
in every human being,
however they behave towards me.

Make possible the impossible
by cultivating in me
the fertile seed of healing love.

May I play my part in breaking the cycle of violence
by realizing that
peace begins with me.

St Ethelburga's Centre for Reconciliation and Peace, England

Home

These bricks have seen
the simple scenes
of loving with its unexpected
and expected ecstasies and fears
like spiders' webs
one moment prisoning our lives
then suddenly a splash of diamonds
in the morning light.
Outside the children
mellowed daylong hours away
oblivious to war.
Last night that home
was swatted
like a fly
bombed
blown to bits
by some strange
stranger in the sky.
My God, my God,
you say that I must love him.
Why?

Harry Wiggett, South Africa

When terrorism scars our lives

When terrorism scars our lives,
in spite of calls to peace;
when governments are callous, deaf,
and, warring, will not cease,
forgetting that the world we share
is only ours on lease;

When innocence and charity
are lost in seamless flame,
when bodies strew our empty streets
and law enforcers maim;
what can we do to wash away
the horror and the shame?

For where is God? And can we hear
The still small voice of calm,
above the din and dissidence,
the cries of our alarm?
And can we ever risk the loss
of face to end this harm?

O give us strength to realize
the love we saw you live
when, in the name of Jesus Christ,
you suffered to forgive
the ones who sought to take your life;
God, show us how to give.

Suggested tune: Revere

Andrew Pratt, England

We are all wounded

Peace makers
Peace breakers
Peace builders
Peace bringers

those who objected,
those who fought,
those who waited at home,
those who worked at home,
those who maimed,
those who feared,
those who killed,
those who defended,
those who wept,

they were all wounded.
We are all wounded.
God, wounded healer,
we name our war-peace stories
we pray our war-peace stories.

those who stayed,
those who strayed,
those who went,
those who were sent,
those who were sacrificed,
those who remember,

they were all wounded.
We are all wounded.
God, wounded healer,
we name our war-peace stories
we pray our war-peace stories.

We are yearning for your living,
we are yearning for your ways on earth,
that we may all be released in peace
yet with scars of wounds of war.

God help us see with the complexities of war.
God help us to live with the wounds of war,
praying and working for its end so the whole world will rejoice.

Kate Gray, England

A prayer in the war

God who gives life,
give life to our war-wasted world.
When our powerful technology gives us power
of life and death, remind us of other powers.
Remind us of the courage it takes to remain truly human
amidst the horror and the enemy.
Remind us of the love it takes to watch and wait for news
of loved ones sent far away into harm.
Remind us of the struggle it takes to stay alive
when water runs out and homes are under fire.
Remind us of the commitment it takes to bring aid
and healing where war has raged.
Remind us of the vision it takes
to lead the nations out of war.
And show us what it means to act upon
the words of Jesus, your Son,
who came to teach and heal and save us.
Show us what the world can become
when we let you lead us. Amen.

Neil Thorogood, England

A prayer for life and love

Lord,
by prayerful offering
and heartfelt loving,
may earth and heaven,
flesh and spirit,
human and divine
combine to create
a communion of life
and love that lasts
for ever.
Amen.

Andrew Clitheroe, England

169

The olive tree and the fig tree

It is Holy Week in this place called the Holy Land. In fact, it is Maundy Thursday, the day we remember the Lord's last supper. It is also Pesach, or Passover, for the Jews. When I become fed up or feel as though nothing I can do will make a bit of difference, as though all my work is in vain, I set out to walk the hills. From where I live it has become more and more difficult to do that. There are two huge, new Jewish settlements that have been established on the hills surrounding Beit Safafa, the Palestinian neighbourhood where I live just outside Bethlehem. A six-lane highway connects Jerusalem with the larger settlements to the east and south. As the checkpoints and the route of the Wall gouge further and further into the West Bank, more and more Palestinians lose access to their fields, to their olive groves and orchards, to their grapevines and grazing land, becoming prisoners in their own homes. Travel on this six-lane highway is forbidden to them. It is only built to ease the way for Jewish settlers who travel from their homes in the huge settlement blocks that expand farther and farther from the centre of Jerusalem to their jobs in the city.

In order to access the quiet hills nearby I need to cross this heavily travelled six-lane highway. Along the way there are two trees, one an olive and one a fig, that have forced their way up through the concrete and stone, rooting themselves stubbornly and fastidiously along this main road as if to remind people, 'I am here. I have been here for centuries. Even your concrete can not kill me!'

I have taken a personal interest in these poor trees. Maybe it's because in a world of so much concrete and stone, I delight in their greenery. Maybe it's because I've always been one to fight for the 'underdog'. Whatever the reason, I look forward to seeing these trees on my walk. Despite their harsh and unaccommodating environment they use whatever means possible to maintain their foothold in the soil. The fig tree has even pushed out some small fruits that will someday feed the birds that stop to rest among its branches. These trees are not full or lush as they should be. The olive tree looks bent and battered, a testament to its short, hard life. These two trees have become symbols for me. Their references in the Bible do not go unremembered. They are part of the landscape here. It is only natural that they appear many times in the Hebrew scriptures, and that Jesus used them in his parables. They are familiar to the people who work the land. They are lovingly cared for and nurtured. They produce fruits that help sustain life. The olive and fig trees have been present in this land for thousands of years, just as the Palestinians have.

On this evening as I walk home past these two trees there is the smell of the lamb roasting on the grill as my Palestinian neighbours remember the Last

Supper. I think of the Palestinians, a people who, like the trees, are rooted in this land; a people whose hospitality and generosity is well known; a people who have persisted in their struggle for survival despite inhuman treatment, despite a broken economy, despite their imprisonment behind concrete walls. They are like the olive and the fig trees. They will survive despite the harsh realities. Their roots go deep and they will struggle until they can bear fruit, until they can once again produce a society that is lush and full, that has an abundance they can share with the world. Their persistence to maintain their dignity in a reality that is crueller than the concrete that surrounds these poor trees is an inspiration for me, just as these two trees bring me hope.

After all, God did not call us to be successful. He called us to be persistent.

Janet Lahr Lewis, United Methodist Missionary in Palestine

There's no peace

There's no peace
there's no peace
always fighting always writhing
no one puts down their guns
only dropping bombs.
But Love alone can heal the wounds caused by greed:
greed for more,
greed for money,
greed for war:
will it stop?
Always bustling, people rushing never stopping

waiting

pausing

to think just what might happen next but always fighting
instead of loving, living, caring.

What will we do in the next minute that may change the world?
God, empower us to learn your peace, shape your peace, share your peace.
Amen.

Kate Gray, England

Promise of hopefulness, pardon and peace

Promise of hopefulness, pardon and peace;
source of deliverance, blessed release;
ground of our being, of darkness and light,
love's possibility, enmity's night;

Cleave to the centre of selfish desire,
bring to creation by earth, wind or fire
all that is hoped for and all that's unseen:
goodness and glory are more than a dream.

In our absurdity, clamour and war
unseat our certainty, counter and floor
all sense of prejudice, hatred and then
offer us strangers that we can befriend.

Give us the courage to enter this cleft,
healing the hurt of the lost, the bereft,
offering hope, though our love's crucified,
soaking up malice where peace is denied.

Love is the answer to vengeance and wrath,
going on loving in spite of the loss,
facing the depth of depravity's gain,
burning our hatred on love's sweeter flame.

Pour out your spirit, God, fill up our lives,
offering loveliness, love that survives,
then take and lift us and raise up our song:
love is yet greater than all human wrong.

Andrew Pratt, England

24/7 world news

24/7 news broadcasting
real-time footage
from behind enemy lines;
podcasts downloaded
to view at convenience
web-blogs offering instant comment
from Joe public;
mobile phones bleep
with the latest news bulletin:
the signs of the times.

So much devastating news
so many real-life tragedies
so much intrusion into
    personal stories
so little respect for human dignity;
an overwhelming flow of pain
a tidal wave of need
an unheard clamour of injustice;
the occasional feel good story
to give us a glimmer of hope:
the signs of the times.

An overload of information
a din of words and pictures
each trying to make an impact
to captivate our attention
so we don't flick channels
or switch off and complain of
    compassion fatigue;
we become desensitized
numb to the pain depicted
    on our screens
unable to ask the unasked questions:
the signs of the times.

The signs of the times
are real-life people:
grandparents, mothers, fathers
children and grandchildren
cities, towns and villages
homes filled with colour
and the knickknacks we can't
    throw away;
laughter and tears
joy and pain
birth and death.

God of all time,
help us to read the signs of the times
to feel the emotions of human stories
the pain of family lives torn apart
the horror and ugliness of conflict
the joy of creativity and achievement
the hope of birth and children playing
the laughter and celebration of a
    beautiful world.
We pray for the people behind the
    media attention;
help us not only to read but to feel
    the signs of the times.

Clare McBeath, England

A prayer in memory of Samir Ibrahim Salman

(Bell ringer at the Church of the Nativity, Bethlehem)

He loved to climb the tower and clang the bell
in Bethlehem, where Jesus Christ was born.
Chimes for the times: he knew them oh-so-well.
He tried to ring again on mayhem morn.

The cave (or manger site) is down below,
where pilgrims kneel to pray their pious fill.
Our bellman climbed the stairs. He didn't know
the hour had come to kill and counter-kill.

Samir was just a simple soul, of course.
The weary watching sniper held his breath
and put his trust in skilled and deadly force.
A shot rang out. The bellman bled to death.

Christ in the crib, he rang the bells for you.
Forgive. We gunmen know not what we do.

John Coutts, England

Manchurian cranes

(Symbol of peace, happiness and longevity
in Japanese art and culture)

Over the island of Hokkaido 900 red-crowned cranes,
with necks measuring the heavens, parasol towards earth.

A singing of cold wings descending;
miracle of legs offering impressions
on the sanctity of snow.
Recomposing a diffusion of light,
stunning ice with virgin steps.
Their sovereign heads rising
to astonish the world.

Eve Jackson, England

Power surge

(7 July 2005)

My daughter calls me
at three in the afternoon.
'You didn't know I was in London
today, did you?'
'No.' My heart misses a beat.

'They said it was a power surge.
We had to be evacuated at
    Bank station.
No one was panicking,
just sitting quietly, doing their
    crosswords.
I couldn't use the phone;
didn't know where I was,
had to walk miles to Vauxhall
to take the train home.'

Her voice sounds so small;
I want to gather her in my arms.
On Friday I buy her gifts,
the usual weekly trivia;
hand soap to rinse the city grime,
herbal bubble-bath to soak away
the stress of that unforgettable day.

Denise Bennett, England

Lead us from war to peace, from death to life

Passionate God,
giver of life and bearer of pain,
we behold you
in the green of the grass
and the lush of the earth,
in the glow of the sun
and the warmth of the rain.
So uphold your harvest people
long held in the grip of hunger
and the terror of war,
in the chill of darkness,
and the shadow of death.
Through the cross of Christ,
lead them from fear to trust,
that swords turn to ploughshares
and spears to pruning hooks.
Guide them from despair to hope
that war cries turn to field songs
and death throes to birth pangs;
and nourish them with the milk
    of peace
that seeds of grace take root
and death give way to life. Amen.

Annabel Shilson-Thomas/
CAFOD, England

175

Peace work

It's hard work, this peace business!
War is easy enough – just pick up a weapon
and charge away at the enemy.
Works for nations and guns
for neighbours and angry words
for my inner being and self-contempt.
Yes, it's not easy.
Not pretty, not gentle, but easy.

Peace, though, that's a different story!
Getting alongside an active warmonger
takes determination.
To stand between two warring factions
takes gut level courage.
To maintain one's own inner peace
non-judgemental objectivity and discerning wisdom
takes more than most of us possess.

And yet that is my calling from God –
possible only by my calling upon his resources,
and working hard at it by his grace.
It's so much easier to hurl a hand-grenade
than build a bridge over the same dividing chasm.
Easier, but not the solution.

Peace, Lord, please.

Abigail Joy Tobler, England

A prayer for freedom

Heavenly Father, free us from the bonds that in life hold us in
death and in death will hold us from life. Amen.

Andrew Clitheroe, England

Grant us peace

Grant us peace that will
break our silence in the midst of violence
then prophetic voices shall resonate.

Grant us peace that will
pull us down from the steeple of our pride
then we'll learn to wash each other's feet.

Grant us peace that will
empty us of hate and intolerance
then we'll turn guns into guitars and sing.

Grant us peace that will
Shut our mouths up when we speak too much
Then we'll learn to listen and understand
What others are saying.

Grant us peace that will
disturb our apathy
then we'll dance together under the sun.

Grant us peace that will
burn our weary hearts
then we'll let love and justice glow. Amen.

Lei Garcia, The Philippines

Symbolic

Strange survivor of the Somme
rusting on my shelf for years,
grinding a small crown of misery
inside my head.

Barbed restrictions, imprisonment –
curtailing my thoughts, accepting life as this.

Today, I decorate in lamb's wool, horsehair and ribbons of waste.
Remembering my own responsibility to lift hope into the light
is sometimes all it takes.

Eve Jackson, England

Peace in Asia

For homeless children
begging in the streets of Colombo,
close to a million internally displaced Burmese,
prostituted women
waiting under Bangkok night lights,
church people and peace advocates
killed in the Philippines:
We pray for peace.

For the victims of war-torn East Timor,
Tuvalu and Kiribati threatened by rising sea levels
because of global warming,
the alarming rate of suicide incidents in Tokyo,
sexually abused migrant workers in Singapore:
We pray for peace.

For factory workers receiving low wages in Beijing,
the long-standing rift in the Korean peninsula,
oppressed and persecuted Dalits in India,
refugees starving to death in Afghanistan:
We pray for peace.

For tsunami victims in South Asia,
troubled relationships between Taiwan and China,
babies born without eyes in Saigon
because of Agent Orange,
brothels filled with thousands of child sex slaves
in Cambodia:
We pray for peace.

We pray for peace
so that carpenters building rich people's houses
will have roofs over their heads,
the life-giving earth will bless us with its fruits,
farmers, whose tears and blood have watered the
fields, will have food on their tables,
textile workers will clothe their weary bodies,
and those who struggle for peace will find justice,
because Christ is our peace.
Amen.

Lei Garcia, The Philippines

Fear

Fear
curls me like a foetus, tight upon myself,
surrounded by impenetrable darkness:
a chrysalis confined
within the hardness of a living tomb.

Time passes
marked only by the thudding of my heart.
From far away I hear familiar sounds:
voices that speak to comfort, tend, advise,
in language that I know, but cannot comprehend.

Sometimes I dream my tears are all wept dry
until a treacherous rip-tide floods across my shore,
and drowns me in its salt-embittered waves.

Will the day come – will it ever come
when I shall turn my face towards the light
and feel, far off, and scarcely recognized,
the first faint stirring of desire to be reborn?
And with my courage stretched to breaking point
shatter this shell of self-doubt and despair,
absolve the past and turn to face a future
where hope will stir again, and wonder beckon,
and joy, with gentle steps, invade my solitude,
and love, which never let me loose into oblivion,
bring me to life again.

Jill Jenkins, England

A Christmas prayer

Holy Christmas peace
seems rather thin
when terror stalks
despite of him.

Bombs and jingle bells
drown out the sound
of God made man
in Jesus found.

So help me to know
as church bells chime
this birth of his
is also mine.

Andrew Clitheroe, England

Lord of darkness and light

Lord of darkness and light,
penetrate our hidden lives
that we may find light in the darkness
and truth in the shadows.
When our hearts are heavy
touch them with your presence
that we may glimpse your glory
and radiate your love.
In suffering and in joy
let your voice be heard,
O chosen Son of God. Amen.

Annabel Shilson-Thomas/CAFOD, England

Chapter Eight

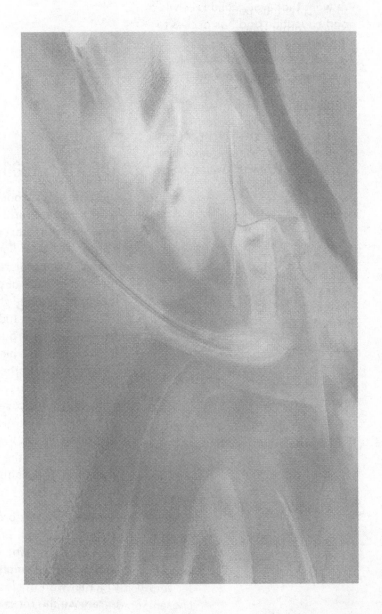

Weaving life

Every child

We want that every child receives a good education and has access to information.
We wish that disabled children receive special medical and economical support and good education.

UNICEF Children's Forum of the International Year of Mountains 2002, Grindelwald, Switzerland

Wintry poem

Silver playground
Silver cars
Frosty bottles

Sparkly grass
Silver trees
White leaves
Patterns on windows

A nine year old child, Down2Earth, Down's Syndrome Association

The rocky road

Virupakshi is a young boy who lives near a remote rural town in the drought prone part of northern Karnataka State, South India. His left leg was paralyzed at the age of three as a result of polio. He was luckier than many children in the area because an India Non-Governmental Organization (NGO) had a clinic near his home town of Deodurg. His mother was taught basic physiotherapy exercises at the clinic to help release the contractures in his leg. Once this was done his family bought him a caliper made at the NGO workshop. This enabled him to walk independently.

Virupakshi's next problem was getting to school, since the road from his house was very rocky. Undeterred, his mother got together with the local community to remove the rocks and make the road safe for her son.

Virupakshi's ambition is to be a doctor.

Ruth Patil, South India/England

A useful member of her community

The best time for Mudamma, a young woman who is married with a young baby, is festival time. She is able to earn extra money for her family as a result of her sewing skills. Mudamma was 12 when she came into contact with the Indian NGO (see opposite). She was living with polio but over the course of seven years she benefited greatly from advice, support, surgery, physiotherapy and later a vocational training course. As a result she was equipped with tailoring skills which are very useful in her remote village community. Mudamma lives one kilometre from the centre of the village and it is not easy for her to trek across the barren, rocky terrain to meet the villagers. She often looks after her baby by herself. When the rains fail and the crops do not grow her husband has to migrate to towns or cities to earn money. Sometimes there is no work so it is important for Mudamma to use her skills to make saris.

Geoffrey Duncan, South India/England

Outside

The kid in my class – **outside** – because he says stupid things, has dull clothes.

Outside because she works too hard and shows off.

Outside because they move around: travelling people, refugee people, people who are trafficked.

Outside because they behave oddly, socially challenged people, not able to cope with the complexity of all the information.

Outside because they do not want to be inside; those who do not need us, do not want the message we bring, know all the answers.

Outside because they are in hospital, residential home/school; those who are forced to wear the label 'patient'.

Lord, enfold us all in your love and at the end welcome us home.

Lesley Charlton, England

183

The blessing of the bizarre

I had a weekly appointment at a high school. I would arrive just as the pupils were leaving for the day. The school provided something of an alternative education for young people who have had difficulty settling at one of the more traditional schools. There is no school uniform.

The appearance of these young people was something of a shock! The girls, in particular, wear astonishing ensembles: some with long, usually black skirts to the floor, others wearing miniskirts, tights and boots; often underwear would be worn on the outside. Boys and girls have hair either long and dyed bright colours or shaven off altogether. Almost everyone is decorated with rings: pierced through ears, nostrils, eyebrows, lips, navel, sometimes tongue! As the weeks passed, however, I began to see these youngsters differently. I got to know some of them. I discovered they are on the whole pleasant and polite, sometimes happy, sometimes sad like everyone in their age group. I began to delight in the imagination and flair revealed in the way they dress. I rejoiced in their freedom from slavery to the dress conventions which, though petty, are strong in the community.

The vision of the Pharisees persists and oppresses yet. We can rejoice in the blessing of God's love for the individuality of each and every person.

John Hunt, Aotearoa New Zealand

Father, who are you?

Father, dad, daddy . . . Father,
where are you, Father?
Father, where are you?
Father, listen to me.

Now, talk to me,
talk to me your son.
Father, talk to me now,
Father, tell me who you are.

Listen, talk to me, Father,
who are you, Father, where have you been?
I've seen you all my life, but who are you?
Father, dad, daddy . . . Father.

Show me the wounds of your journey through life,
those lines on your hands, you cannot hide.
Father, I see your life in your eyes,
but show me how you have lived.

Why don't you show me your heart?
Why do you hide behind your armour?
Fail to tell me the tale those eyes portray,
those eyes that have cried, but never with me.

If I never know you, who am I?
What is a man without knowing his father?
He's like a child with a stranger, the child's still alone,
a lonely life for both to suffer.

So let me in, show me your face,
show me your heart and your wounds.
Let me see your tears and your smile,
then show me your spirit and soul,

Then one day, I will say, 'I know my father,
I know where he's been and I know who he is,
I'll know where he's gone,
and I know the place he is now.'

Michael Watson, England

The high bed

We were like dregs
in a cup;
living in a damp basement flat.

A dungeon
with one window
where we watched the legs go by.

Coming up for air
our arms would scoop the sun,
eyes squinting at the iris sky.

At night we slept
in the high bed;
my brother and I,

slipped between the sheets
like precious trinkets
into an envelope, sealed with a kiss.

By day I would scoot
the gloomy rooms,
one limb tucked under.

My mother told me
I was as good as gold,
never made a sound,

but waited by the door
in the dark, to watch
the light flutter down.

Denise Bennett, England

Sick child

Small you lie,
diminished within your frame,
wisp-like on undented fleece
in weightless patience
hovering –
time suspends you,
day long,
night long
In tideless ripple . . .
Do you skim on the surface
or sink like the silk-smooth stone
to the pool-dark depths?
In all your quiet watching
do you see the needle's eye?
Is paradise there
in sun and skipping
beyond your tube-tethered world?

You will not be lost –
for if you pass through
'tis only your present is gone –
your future and past will
    seamless unite,
and the thread of your life
will reassure our continuity.

Margot Arthurton, England

Grounds Celebration Day

(When children create paperponds)

You have to be
knee high to a child's wonder
to view these petal shaped ponds
– made in celebration of all things –
to appreciate the way they magnify the world
and how small children see larger than us.

Pause in their stillness, down
where the roots drink in the hush of summer,
where dragonflies settle on the still gaze
of the day; iridescent wings netting
the light. Goldfish swirl and curl with gentle ease,
nodding lily pads and reeds; water and weed
stirring beneath. The grassy banks
where folded frogs only just hold on to their leaps.

Eve Jackson, England

One wonders

One wonders, Lord, if you have a low self-esteem,
experiencing rejection all your life,
needing praise as much or more as some of us.

One wonders, Lord, if you have a negative self-image,
experiencing belittlement as you matured,
needing affirmation as much or more as some of us.

One wonders, Lord, if you have a saviour-complex,
experiencing others' needs all your life,
needing attention as much or more as some of us.

One wonders, Lord, if you have a traumatized Inner Child
experiencing opposition from your birth,
needing loving as much or more as some of us.

Frances Ballantyne, England

Siblings

Not Esau, serious-minded and honest,
but young Jacob, with his cunning and deceit;

not Eliab or Abinadab or any of the faithful brothers
serving at the unexpected sacrifice
there when called on,
but David, bright, attractive, the youngest,
overlooked, out with the sheep;

not Leah, plain and so painfully substituted
to overcome the shame of the younger
sister marrying first,
but Rachel, more beautiful,
so beautiful that Jacob is willing to wait,

and the prodigal, the wasteful,
careless of his father and family,
causing anguish and chaos,
he is the chosen, the symbol of new life,
not the elder brother, always there,
outside now, looking in with unwished for jealousy
that hurts so much.

Always the younger, youngest,
Holy Writ and Fairy Tale.
Has anyone got anything to say to the older sibling?
Anything to offer but faithfulness, endurance
and unrequited love?

Janet Wootton, England

Looking-glass generation

Cover those first threads of silver
and rub in miraculous creams.
Abolish those dread Signs of Ageing
if you want to accomplish your dreams.

The dermatological clinic
will deal with that wrinkle or line.
Succumb to the knife or the needle
and life will continue just fine.

That cannot be cellulite showing!
You're working so hard to keep slim.
So try out the latest fad diet.
Spend three days a week in the gym.

And then everybody will love you.
Forget that the looking glass lies,
and imagine that smooth mask of beauty
is hiding the pain in your eyes.

Father God, you created us as we are and our faces become etched with the
realities of our living. May we be loved for what is within us. Help us to see
beyond the masks that others present to the world.

Christine Ractliff, England

Remembering

Spaces of movement
warm, tender, snug;
curled within,
memories persist.

> *'I have made you,*
> *I have formed you within*
> *the womb.' (Isa. 44.2)*

Heartbeats resound
following their own rhythms into life.
Echoes uniting,
'Hold me close, mama',
penetrating again
that haven of tranquillity.

> *'I have carried you,*
> *since the time you were born.'*
> *(Isa. 44.3)*

Man and woman
lining each other in the quiet dark
in collective consciousness
of the Divine receptacle,
soaking up the gyan[1] of love
to linger on and nourish in separation.

> *'See, I have carved you*
> *on the palms of my hands.'*
> *(Isa. 49.16)*

Foetal positions:
insecure, depressed.
weighed down by life's choices
or lack of them;
crouched in fear
shutting out the violence and terror
seeking natal comfort
before the loss of all humanity.

> *'Does a woman forget her baby*
> *at the breast*
> *or the mother the child within*
> *her womb?*

> *Yet even if these forget,*
> *I will never forget my own.'*
> *(Isa. 49.15)*

Incarnated,
embodied,
Divine Seed
nestled in a woman's womb.

Created in one image,
cosmic cycle complete.

> *'Unto us a child is born.'*

> *Astrid Lobo Gajiwala, India*

1 Gyan (Sanskrit): knowledge, to know with one's whole being, more often used for spiritual knowledge.

The womb is a place of security to which we unconsciously return, again and again – a little child sitting on a mother's lap wanting to be held close, almost pushing to get back into the womb, to be physically one again; partners charging each other's emotional batteries in the physical closeness of sleeping within each other; human beings in the face of life's battering finding solace in foetal positions reminiscent of the safety of the womb, human and divine. It is to this womb that God entrusts God's child, cosmic connections embodied in human flesh, recalling Yahweh who holds us within the divine womb and gives birth to the divine image.

Son

So you are come . . .
Flushed on a flood tide
from the mystic cave
you tumble into life;
with your wild primeval cry
you speak for all the earth
in secret wordlessness –
old truths that will be lost
within the knowledge of your growing . . .
And at the flow of life
you consummate with knowing greed
the need of every child,
and stake the claim
of every man
upon the breast
of womanhood . . .
And then, so satisfied,
you lie, cave-shaped
and sleeping . . . every breath
sustained within the keeping
of a promise
that is immortality.

Margot Arthurton, England

Excluded

Excluded from the garden.
Excluded from the room.
Distant voices sing and dance in a circle
Women meeting making connections
Breaking down barriers
Excluded from the room.

Where are the women?
They should be here
Is our agenda not their agenda?
Is my agenda not my sisters'?
It is easily dismissed.
Excluded from the room.

Where are the women?
The blind, the deaf
The women in chairs
Women who hate deep flights of stairs
Physical barriers get in the way
Of spiritual intent
Excluded from the room.

Is my cross not your cross?
How can we meet?
Me with my wheels
You with your feet
How will we find out?
Excluded from the room.

Excluded from the well
It made a pleasant change
Usually they take me there
To put me in the water
Hoping for a miracle
To reverse the damage

Excluded from the garden.
Excluded from the room.

Jean Palmer, England

middle-classness

Spare me your tranquil self-righteousness,
your glib, cheery clichés crashing,
shattering hollow and empty. Disrobe!
Take off that off-the-shelf personality.

Then tell me true tales
of your most noble failures,
courageous questionings,
and hesitant convictions.

Who knows?
I may glimpse an incarnate God,
or the vague, lingering scent of a passing.

Robert Bos, Australia

Creator of bodies

God of queer and straight and dyke,
boldly love with us as we do.
God of wrinkles, grey hairs and laughter lines,
boldly love with us as we do.
God of scar tissue, saggy bodies and stitches,
boldly love with us as we do.

God of love,
creator of bodies,
we will remake your world through our bodies of loving,
we will remake your world through your love; our love. Amen.

Kate Gray, England

Wild child

Will I tell my mother I can mother too?
I cannot, for the child she sees in me
is still wild, and waiting to be tamed –
she sees me ungrown yet
and framed in childhood . . .

How can I tell her that I know
the secrets of my own conception?
That all her veiled warnings
came too late? That passion's spate
engulfed me like a flood
more brilliant than blood?

And now my inner childhood quite
abandons me,
and from a moment's gasp
gives life and separation
to another inner child in secret . . .

She will know of course –
for she has instincts too,
and may abandon me.
I am not ready for that yet.
So shall I grow this child,
or kill it?
In so doing will I perpetuate
abandonment so dreaded in my heart
upon this inner child and all who follow it?

I search my mind
and find no answer there –
no kind solution.
Only retribution
wished upon another life.

For whom I am unready.

Margot Arthurton, England

Grace is on the loose

Grace is on the loose
for us.

We:
tittle-tattlers and tarts
do-gooders and drunkards
over-pious and prejudiced
the fearful and the frivolous
the violent and the violated
politically correct and pompous
the arrogant and the abused
the deniers and the delirious.
Grace is on the loose for us, for all of us.
Alleluia! Amen.

Kate Gray, England

Help us liberate . . .

God,
   decolonize our minds and our churches.
   Help us liberate scriptures and find our faith freed in the process.

God,
   decolonize our motivations and our private lives.
   Help us liberate sexuality and find our love freed in the process.

God,
   decolonize our consumerism and our shopping.
   Help us liberate economics and find our trading freed in the process.

Amen.

Kate Gray, England

Let me be

(A homosexual's plea to parts of the Church)
I have no evil demons
for you to exorcise.
I am who I am.
Don't label me with lies.

Don't rant and rave of choices
not on offer to me.
I am who I am.
Why can't you let me be?

Don't condemn me as sinful.
Don't say I am depraved.
I am who I am.
I refuse to be 'saved'.

Don't abuse your religion
to load guilt onto me.
I am who I am
with the right to be free.

Blind guides, why must you persist
in this hypocrisy?
I am who I am,
as God created me.

My prayer

Living God, Essence of Being,
Great 'I AM',
do not let my difference
be a stumbling block
to those who fear it;
do not let their fear
be unjustly focused on me.
Open their eyes,
that they may see
not our points of difference,
but our shared humanity. Amen.

Jean Mortimer – for Matthew and many friends, England

Christmas cactus

(For Emily and Charlene on their forthcoming partnership)

This first year
was a bit hit and miss –
forgive me.

I didn't know
you needed rain water
and an east facing window sill;

didn't realize how
your succulent stems
would burst into coral flame

scalding the frosty air,
how they would warm me
this Christmas day.

Didn't know how you would remind me
of my nocturnal daughter;
the dormant years

when she slept day long
always waking in darkness
to slake her thirst.

I might have guessed
she would plan a November nuptial,
late afternoon, the time

when winterlight weaves
an early dusk,
when red stars litter the lawn.

A time when she will take
the girl with the midnight hair
in her arms,

and you will bloom again
unfurling your wedding petals
to bless their vows.

Denise Bennett, England

Single bliss

'It's easier for you,' they said,
'Having no family.'
They mean, of course, I'm free, not cluttered up
With other people's problems.
My house, once tidied, stays that way,
Without the trail of toys and cast-off
Clothing up the stairs, the muddy footmarks
And the tide-marked bath.
Food's left for its intended purpose, not
Picked at by impatient hands, or
Prematurely eaten.

If that is what life's for, it's easier.
But outward order does not bring content.
Realities of life lie in relationships,
And at the heart of singleness one is
Alone.
Of course, the barren women do keep house,*
No one will do it for them. But to be a
Joyful mother, one always has to borrow
Someone else's children.

Psalm 113.8

Ann Lewin, England

forgetting

At first, he laughed it off.
Lapses of memory.
'A senior's moment' he called it.

Names escaped him.
His glasses were lost.
Had he showered that morning?

'Alzheimer's' they called it.
Dementia. A one word sentence.
Little by little his soul leaked out.

'Who are you, dear?'
'I'm Janie, your daughter!'
'Ooooh. That's nice, dear.'

Robert Bos, Australia

The man who shouts

The man who shouts in the street
is scary;
we are wary of him,
and in our fear
keep clear.

For he is other
in some curious way
we cannot understand –
and so we brand him
unapproachable.

Why do we fear his shouting?
For he sees us not;
sees only demons in his
inner world.
For he is quite curled in
upon himself
alone –
for demons are no company . . .
And so we leave him
battling there –
battling . . .

How can we do this?

Margot Arthurton, England

Fragments from a shattered mind

Fragments of memories
pass through my mind
disjointed, disconnected
disorientating me.

Each fragment is sharp
piercing the heart
each remembered pain
or joy, or fear
brings history near.

And my shattered mind
cannot cope
with the barrage of emotion
causing commotion
increasing revulsion
in me
for me
and my shattered mind.

The fragments have no sequence
no logical link
For a moment I'm six
then twenty-two or -three
now married, now divorced
till in the end I cannot see
who is the real me.

Fragments, fragments, fragments
whirling around
whirling me round
confusing my confusion
shattering my sanity
resisting reality
fragments that's all that's left of me.

A.K. Heathcoat, England

Ostinato staccato

I've got a rhythm in my head
'You'd be better off dead'
It's a rhythm like a train
A constant refrain
Ostinato
Staccato
'You'd be better off dead
After what you've said
You'd be better off dead.'

It's there all the time
A rhythm, a rhyme
Though the train changes line
Though my thoughts lose time
Ostinato
Staccato
'You'd be better off dead
Why bother living?
You'd be better off dead!'

'You've broken a marriage
Ruined a life'
Ostinato
Staccato
'You'd be better off dead.'

'You've told fairy stories
Believed in lies'
Ostinato
Staccato
'You'd be better off dead.'

'You've turned them against him
You've lied about him'
Ostinato
Staccato
'You'd be better off dead.'

'You're just a pest and a problem
No one wants you around'
Ostinato
Staccato
'You'd be better off dead.'

'You only cause trouble
You want your own way'
Ostinato
Staccato
'You'd be better off dead.'

'You will not be missed
Better dead than alive'
Ostinato
Staccato
'You'd be better off dead.'

'Retain your dignity
Release him from hell'
Ostinato
Staccato
'You'd be better off dead.'

The rhythm in my brain
The rhythm of the train
A voice in my head
'You'd be better off dead.'
Ostinato
Staccato
'You'd be better off dead.
You'd Be Better Off Dead.
YOU'D BE BETTER OFF DEAD.'

I'd be better off dead.

A Survivor, England

So many times

So many times,
I would like to say 'Yes, I can.'
But instead I say 'No, I can't.'
I'd like to believe that I could
    manage,
but don't trust myself to cope,
I don't trust myself not to go wrong.
I might make a mess,
or upset others.

So many times,
I would like to say 'Yes, I can.'
But instead I say 'No, I can't.'
I know I used to be able to do it,
but now I can't remember how,
or my failing body may let me down.
I might make a mess,
or upset others.

So many times,
I would like to say 'Yes, I can.'
But instead I say 'No, I can't.'
I haven't the courage to do
    what's required,
I can't face doing it alone,
I'm too shy, unhappy and afraid.
I might make a mess,
or upset others.

So many times,
I would like to say 'Yes, I can.'
But instead I say 'No, I can't.'
I simply haven't the time,
to stop and help others, or me,
and if I do it in a hurry
I might make a mess,
or upset others.

So many times,
I have said 'Yes, I can,'
when I was tempted to say
    'No, I can't.'
And what joy I got out of the work!
Although I was shy and wary,
the Lord gave me strength
    and courage;
I may have made a mess,
or upset others,
but his love always shone through.

A.K. Heathcoat, England

202

They cannot get in

They pick him up on a stretcher,
carry him into the sun.
Straining as they carry him up on the roof.
Family members caring for a disabled family member.

Disabled people longing for independence.
Neighbours who allow someone to stay in their home
because they shop and pop round.

They cannot get in.
There are too many people.
No way through.
Churches designed to keep you, Jesus,
for themselves,
to keep strangers out.
Churches that are clubs of the like-minded.
Making needy people feel humiliated
and thinking somehow of God as a pet.

Your sins are forgiven.
Many cannot hear these words.
People burdened by guilt.

Get up and walk.
Those who find movement too demanding
want to stay where they are.

Lord Jesus,
may you be at home with us
and may we make room
in our structures
and personalities for you.

Lesley Charlton, England

The holding

Don't tell me I'll get better
in a month or two or three;
tell me your love is strong enough
to embrace this raw and real me.

Don't tell me you'll support me
on a long and wearing road;
I don't want to travel your way
with your love as my goad.

Don't tell me about how proud you are
or say 'Just look how far you've come';
as if travelling is the only thing
and perfection the only home.

Don't treat me like a small child
whose hurt can be cuddled away;
but treat me like an adult
and listen to what I say.

I don't want to be someone else's shape
or to be squashed into another's frame;
I want to know it's me you love
with all my joys and shame.

I need to feel when I'm with you
however I may be;
that I am treasured as I am,
not as some future perfect me.

A.K. Heathcoat, England

Auntie Joyce

In my conservatory
I tend the plants I've grown to love,
bougainvillea, gloxinia,
the blood-red geraniums . . .

think of my aunt, her funeral,
when I learnt that in all her 86 years
she had never left Devon,
never been further than Exeter.

Today I recall the familiar lane
to her cottage, her neat garden
the way she took me in
when I was weeks old;

how she brought me on
like a broken stem in a glass of water;
helped me to put down
my first tender roots.

Denise Bennett, England

Stroke

I've never seen her passionate,
only a dry peck,
a quick brush of the cheek,

but each day now
she streaks red lipstick
across her crooked mouth;
puckers up her lop-sided lips, pouts –
and practises giving her husband
of nearly 60 years,
a diamond kiss.

Denise Bennett, England

Home

Mother is so well cared for.
She has a lovely room, her own TV,
a pleasant view, three nice meals a day.
She can even press a buzzer in emergency.

We sit here nodding through the afternoon,
we nuisances who have stayed on too long.
My chair is by the window so I see
the lengthening of shadows day by day.
I am not hungry. We who are tidied carefully away
feast on memories, remember when
our skills were needed and our hands were held.
Now hard-pressed girls, in crispy overalls,
make kind and sympathetic sounds.
Some nights the darkness swallows me.
Fear closes in, around, below, above . . .
I do not call because I know
the buzzer will not bring me love.

Christine Ractliff, England

Loved

She grew most things – but never religion.
Never out-blossomed her space of light. Resisted any handing over,
conforming or following those who ploughed straight lines
day and night. Refused to peddle inheritance,
or chivvy those who were slow. Did not let darkness overshadow
her day. Despaired at smugness that coloured people's eyes. Cared
passionately if saplings weakened, forest flowers were dimmed.
Tendered no bark to be carved. Nurtured all living things.

She was a gardener – rooted in God, discarding seeds
of thought that may have, one day, reached beyond him.
Harvesting the best of moments; healing from each day's bloom.
Weeding out the worst of her self; collecting good deeds
that spread at her feet.

There was stillness in her being; a completeness
of the balmy summer evening. Wanting no more
than to hold a curl of a leaf. Loved the simplest of things.

Eve Jackson, England

206

Bereft

(Reflections on the death of my father)

In the quiet solitude of my room
the tears fall, loving Lord.
Not for dad (he's with you)
for me, in my loneliness.
I've suddenly realized
I'm an orphan – parentless;
unwillingly deserted by the person
who was father and mother
to me for many years.
I've become like a displaced person too
– homeless, as the house I was brought up in
is no longer home; repossessed
by the Council, given away to someone else.

I see now, Lord, why you commanded
your people to care for the orphan and widow,
the stranger, and the dispossessed of the land.
And, as I sort through my father's clothes,
I understand the awful effrontery
of the words: 'They divided
my garments among them.'

Loving God, (I cannot bear
to call you Father at the moment)
I pray for the fatherless, and the widowed,
for the homeless, and the refugees.
I pray for those on endless
housing lists, waiting longingly
for a home to call their own;
for the people stripped of their clothes,
and their dignity, and the others
who haven't even a coat to put on their back.
I pray for the deserted,
and the lonely – everyone waiting
for the footfall which never comes . . .
And, loving parent God,
I pray for me.

Carol Dixon, England

The home

On her ninety-third birthday
they gave her a zimmer frame.
Caged from the waist down
she paces the floor like a tired lion.

Sometimes she takes it in her stride,
bears her bars well;
other times I see her sad animal eyes –
and turn away when she roars.

I watch her courage drain;
these days she mostly sleeps
in her corner –
waiting for her keeper.

Denise Bennett, England

Sunflowers

(For Grandma who died 31 July 2006)
They have come early
this year

thrusting up from poor soil
sunstars rising
from bone-dry earth,

black-eyed beauties
the colour of joy
yellowing the garden.

You would have loved
these sunny heads
climbing to the shining sky;

the way they cluster
like bright, happy children
jostling for attention.

Denise Bennett, England

Uncle's funeral

At your funeral
I sang each little flower that
    opens . . .
It was the first day of spring.

Afterwards I drove
along the coast to Saunton Sands,
your favourite place,

where the sea
was harebell-blue,
and the sky full of pearl.

That was 15 years ago,
today I stake the passion flower,
grown from your cuttting;

touch the violet-haloed heads,
knowing that soon
the sweet fruit will come.

Denise Bennett, England

New candles

New candles.
Satin-smooth, unmarked,
anonymous.
Untouched by life.
Beautiful in unsullied innocence?

Burning candles,
dribbling wax,
Marring pristine beauty?
But, characterful,
individual,
enhanced by the ravages of use.

So with old faces,
etched with life,
no longer satin-smooth anonymity
but characterful,
pages of life's journey,
beautiful images of God.

Ros Murphy, England

In praise of hope

Hope is an unexpected letter:
'Hey, we love you – please get better.'

Hope is a voice from long ago:
ringing up to say 'Hello.'

Hope is a sunlit baby's room,
whose guest is dancing in the womb.

Hope is a young and puzzled brow:
a smile that says 'I get it now.'

Hope turns up to sweep and scrub
when fools have vandalized the club.

Hope takes part in sponsored walks.
Hope puts up with boring talks.

Hope is a well that's truly sunk:
healthy water gladly drunk.

Faith and Love are Jack and Jill;
hope will help them up the hill.

Hope is . . . hope is . . . what you will.

John Coutts, England

Index of authors

Adams, Graham   13, 158
Antone, Hope S.   54, 98, 104
Arthurton, Margot   45, 87, 89, 92, 134, 186, 191, 194, 199

Ball, Brian   166
Ballantyne, Frances   37, 77, 113, 187
Bennett, Denise   61, 175, 186, 197, 205, 208, 209
Birkinshaw, Marie   91
Blowers, Jeanne   14, 17, 18, 81
Bookless, Dave   86
Bos, Robert   84, 114, 193, 199
Bower, Pauline   154, 156
Brookes, Jean   40
Brown, John Adamson   71, 125
Brown, Stephen   53, 160

CAFOD   5
Charlton, Lesley   183, 203
Chivers, Chris   128
Christian Ecology Link   87, 90
Clitheroe, Andrew   26, 47, 52, 63, 78, 79, 80, 122, 124, 169, 176, 180
Constable, Doug   15
Cornick, David   34
Coutts, John   174, 210

Dixon, Carol   66, 67, 207
Dobson, Marjorie   6, 12, 19, 22, 24, 50, 84, 85, 146
Down's Syndrome Association   182
Duncan, Geoffrey   10, 17, 29, 110, 133, 183

Edwards, Martin   90
Esdon, Norm S.D.   23, 38, 162

Fernando, Basil   95, 117

Gajiwala, Astrid Lobo   116, 118, 119, 121, 190
Garcia, Lei   177, 178
Gobledale, Ana   159
Gobledale, Mandla   117
Gobledale, Tod   159
Granahan, Louise Margaret   24
Gray, Kate   4, 14, 16, 18, 37, 67, 68, 72, 82, 101, 112, 113, 115,
                       136, 138, 139, 149, 150, 168, 171, 193, 195
Graystone, Peter   4, 33, 44, 56, 80

Index of titles and first lines

Where the first line of a piece differs from its title, the first line is listed and displayed in italics.

Acknowledgements

Chapter One   **Celebrate our diversity**

Bright wind of heaven, The © Stainer & Bell Ltd.
Broaden our vision © Kate Gray

Christ in ordinary people © David Jenkins
Conversation © Marjorie Dobson
Creed, A © CAFOD

Diverse Ways © Doug Constable
Dyspraxia © Joseph Watson

Embracing © Marjorie Dobson

Forgiving God © Marjorie Dobson

Gathering prayer © Clare McBeath
Guarantees, glory and grit © Marjorie Dobson

Haiku on the Parable of the Lost Sheep © A.K. Heathcoat
Honest Thomas © Norm S.D. Esdon
How do you play dominoes? © Michael Watson

Images of God © Jean Palmer
In the temple © Janet Lees
Inviting all © Graham Adams

Joy of intimacy, The © Annabel Shilson-Thomas/CAFOD

Letting go © Eve Jackson
Lifestyles © Kate Gray
Litany of friendship © A.K. Heathcoat
Loving me? © Jeanne Blowers

My Creed – My Beatitude © Geoffrey Duncan

Praise to you, O God our maker © Peter Graystone
Prayer for renewal © Louise Margaret Granahan
Prayer of confession, A © Sonja Rauchfuss. Used with permission of the World
    Alliance of Reformed Churches

Reflection on rainbows © Kate Gray
Remove all prejudice © Geoffrey Duncan

Soundscapes of the city © Clare McBeath
Spirituality © Jeanne Blowers

Take time © Marjorie Dobson
To be needed © Jeanne Blowers

With you is home © Kate Gray

Chapter Two   . . . that all might learn

And when will the whole world rejoice © Kate Gray

Bearing pain © Abigail Joy Tobler
Beyond Make Poverty History © Annabel Shilson-Thomas/CAFOD
Bring an end to injustice © Peter Graystone
Broken child © M.R. Manohar

Children of a lesser God © M.R. Manohar
Confession © Bob Warwicker

Fairer world, A © Elizabeth Smith
Find room © Marjorie Dobson

Go forth from this place © Hope S. Antone
God is dying with the children © Andrew Pratt
God of the waters © Peter Graystone
God's world © Clare McBeath

Illumine our hearts and minds © Annabel Shilson-Thomas/CAFOD

Jesus on the boundaries © John Lansley
Just an ordinary man © Cecily Taylor

Kiss of life, The © Stephen Brown

Living Lord of hope for the world © Geoffrey Duncan

Meditative prayer © David Cornick

Not quite © Eve Jackson

Once more © Abigail Joy Tobler

Parent, forgive © Wendy Whitehead
Petition © Bob Warwicker
Prayer for forgiveness, A © Andrew Clitheroe
Prayer for solidarity, A © Annabel Shilson-Thomas
Prayer for the love of Christ, A © Andrew Clitheroe

Rainbow God © Tim Presswood
Running sores © Margot Arthurton

Song of the vineyard Eucharist © Clare Mc Beath

. . . that the rich might learn from those who are poor © Andrew Clitheroe
Transformation © Ros Murphy

Weaving prayer © Jenny Spouge
What is God worth? © Jenny Spouge
Whole world will rejoice, The (1) © Norm S.D. Esdon
Whole world will rejoice, The (2) © Samia Khoury
Wisdom © Janet Lees
World rejoices, The © Frances Ballantyne
World will rejoice, The © Jean Brookes

Chapter Three   Take hope – know joy – witness justice

Abuse is . . . © A Survivor
Advent dialogue © John Lansley
Another world is possible © Kate Gray

Bits of love © John Adamson Brown, first published in Croydon 'Poets Anonymous'

Compassion © Ann Lewin
Cost of forgiveness, The © Carol Dixon
Cry of the child © Martin Hazell

Dear God you are our future © Vaughan Jones

Empathy © Ros Murphy

First music © Harry Wiggett
Free us to forgive ourselves © Kate Gray

God of all the world © Peter Graystone
God of the broken © A.K. Heathcoat
God, you are a big God © Kate Gray

Hope © Claire Smith

I have called you by your name and you are mine © Janet Wootton

Journey . . . Stations of the Cross, The © Harry Wiggett

Loneliness © A.K. Heathcoat
Love, joy, hope © Heather Johnston

Make your home among us © Annabel Shilson-Thomas/CAFOD
Moulded to Compassion © Jeanne Blowers

No counsellors – please © Denise Bennett, first published in Acumen
No place to go © Fredwyn Hosier

Our own Good Fridays © Carol Dixon

Prayer for forgiving love, A © Andrew Clitheroe
Prayer for humility, A © Andrew Clitheroe
Prayer for suffering love, A © Andrew Clitheroe
Prayer of service to others, A © Andrew Clitheroe

Rage's blood © Frances Ballantyne
Rejection © Fredwyn Hosier

School yard, The © Michael Watson
Send people who are compassionate © Peter Graystone
Someone's life © Kayliegh Kirkham
Special © Ann Lewin
Spirit, free in all the world © Kate Gray
Stories of the children, The © Fredwyn Hosier

TRC (Truth and Reconciliation Commission) © Harry Wiggett

Thankfulness © Andrew Clitheroe
True love © Jeanne Blowers

What am I worth? © Fredwyn Hosier
Whole world will rejoice, The © Joan Heybourne

Chapter Four   Creation – culture – community

Amazing Lord © Christine Ractliff

Birds © Hannah Warwicker
Creation, culture, community © Clare McBeath
Creation Sunday © Dave Bookless

Desert blessing © Clare McBeath

Ecological and economic justice © Tara Tyme. Used with permission of the World
      Alliance of Reformed Churches

Holding the pebble © Marjorie Dobson
Hopes of youth © Janet Lees

I am © David Tutty

King Country mist © Wendy Ward
Kiss of Life © Margot Arthurton

moonlight © Robert Bos

Operation Noah prayer, The © Christian Ecology Link
Our world © Martin Edwards

Prayer about fresh air, A © Basil Fernando
Prayer from the Pacific, A © Rotaiti Kabatiiaa. Used with permission of the World
      Alliance of Reformed Churches
Prayer of commitment © Christian Ecology Link
Prayer of thanksgiving for creation and communion © Kate Gray
Promise © Marjorie Dobson

Rainforest (1) © Christine Ractliff
Rainforest (2) © Eve Jackson
Rainsong © Margot Arthurton
Reckless living – prodigal moments © David Pickering
Rediscovering the rainbow © Marie Birkinshaw
Respecting the earth and its people © Annabel Shilson-Thomas/CAFOD

Separated from Mother Earth © Hope S. Antone in *Unleashing the Power Within Us:
      Meditations for Asian Women*, a booklet jointly produced by Asian Women's
      Resource Centre and other women's groups (Manila 2001), pp. 77–78.
Spirit gives us ears, The © World Alliance of Reformed Churches
Spirit of the living God © Geoffrey Duncan
Spring © Margot Arthurton

Take a walk on the wild side © Hannah Warwicker

Water meter, The © Janet Lees
We celebrate the creation © Hope S. Antone and Corazon Tabing-Reyes

Chapter Five   Moments of grace

Awareness © Janet Lees

Beatitudes for interfaith families © Astrid Lobo Gajiwala
Build Your World © Annabel Shilson-Thomas/CAFOD

Christ in the high street © John Adamson Brown
Compassionate God © Frances Ballantyne
Cross-cultural barriers © Geraldine Witcher

Final suppers © Mandla Gobledale
Freeing God © Astrid Lobo Gajiwala

In the light of a new morning © Eve Jackson
Interfaith worship for peace in the Middle East © Andrew Clitheroe

Lights in the darkness © Chris Chivers
Lily is born © Eve Jackson

Mary meets Buddha's mother © Basil Fernando
Moment of Grace, A © Astrid Lobo Gajiwala

Prayer for blessing, A © Andrew Clitheroe
Prayer of a desperate parent, A © Zam Walker
Presence © Kate Gray

Rainbow spirit © Kate Gray
receive me © Robert Bos

Silence together © Kate Gray
Spice trade © Diana Roberts

We are one © Heather Johnston
We come by many different paths © Stainer and Bell
What has God done in your life? © A.K. Heathcoat

Chapter Six   Set us all free

Asylum seekers © Ann Lewin

Belonging to each other © Clare McBeath
Blood © Wendy Ward
Bring light into dark places © Geoffrey Duncan

Celebrate the Haystack Bicentennial © Ana and Tod Gobledale
Chain, The © Ros Murphy
Country we could share, A © Kate Gray
Cross-dressing God © Kate Gray

Divisions and unity © A.K. Heathcoat

Freedom and unity © Claire Smith

Fugitive, The © Margot Arthurton

God of love, we welcome you © Kate Gray
God of surprises © Graham Adams
God whom we fail to see © Kate Gray

Here stands a stranger, who is she? © Andrew Pratt
Human beings, bought and bartered © Andrew Pratt

Imagine . . . © Clare McBeath
Intercession © Diana Roberts

Litany of repentance and supplication, A © Pauline Bower
Living, loving Father of us all © Pauline Bower

Making a difference © Clare McBeath
'My chains fell off, my heart was free' © John Roberts

No © Janet Wootton

Observer © Janet Lees
Overcoming obstacles © Michael Watson

Portrayal © Eve Jackson
Prayer for the oldest trade in the world © Kate Gray

Rainbow people © Lythan Nevard
Refugees © Ann Lewin

Sale price! © Marjorie Dobson
Security – thanksgiving and confession © Clare McBeath
set all free © 'set all free'

There, there, you'll soon get over it © David Isherwood
Touch the truth © Stephen Brown

We cannot be dismissive © Andrew Pratt
What a way to earn a living © Martin Hazell
Witch and widow © Kate Gray

Chapter Seven   The urgent need for humankind

24/7 world news © Clare McBeath

Atonement © Norm S.D. Esdon

Christmas prayer, A © Andrew Clitheroe

Father, forgive © Rose Reeve
Fear © Jill Jenkins

Grant us peace © Lei Garcia

Home © Harry Wiggett

Lead us from war to peace, from death to life © Annabel Shilson-Thomas/CAFOD
Lord of darkness and light © Annabel Shilson-Thomas/CAFOD

Love one another © Heather Johnston

Manchurian cranes © Eve Jackson

Nageena © Abigail Joy Tobler

Olive tree and the fig tree, The © Janet Lahr Lewis

Peace in Asia © Lei Garcia
Peace work © Abigail Joy Tobler
Power surge © Denise Bennett
Prayer for an end to violence, A © St Ethelburga's Centre for Reconciliation and Peace
Prayer for freedom, A © Andrew Clitheroe
Prayer for life and love, A © Andrew Clitheroe
Prayer in memory of Samir Ibrahim Salman © John Coutts
Prayer in the war, A © Neil Thorogood
Promise of hopefulness, pardon and peace © Andrew Pratt

Symbolic © Eve Jackson

There's no peace © Kate Gray

We are all wounded © Kate Gray
We should not live through this without a protest © Andrew Pratt
When terrorism scars our lives, Andrew Pratt © Stainer and Bell
Will we turn the other cheek? © Brian Ball

Chapter Eight   Weaving life

Auntie Joyce © Denise Bennett

Bereft © Carol Dixon
Blessing of the bizarre, The © John Hunt

Christmas cactus © Denise Bennett
Creator of bodies © Kate Gray

Every child © UNICEF Children's Forum
Excluded © Jean Palmer

Father, who are you? © Michael Watson
forgetting © Robert Bos
Fragments from a shattered mind © A.K. Heathcoat

Grace is on the loose © Kate Gray
Grounds Celebration Day © Eve Jackson

Help us liberate . . . © Kate Gray
High bed, The © Denise Bennett
Holding, The © A.K. Heathcoat
Home © Christine Ractliff
Home, The © Denise Bennett

In praise of hope © John Coutts